Jim Burgen does an amazing job of authentically telling his story and how Jesus helped him break free. You'll want to read *No More Dragons* and discover how you can break free from anything and everything that keeps you from being the person God meant for you to be and to help others do the same.

— Dave Ferguson, lead pastor, Community Christian Church; lead visionary, NewThing

NO
MORE
DRAGONS

NO MORE DRAGONS

DRAGONS

Get Free from Broken Dreams, Lost Hope,

Bad Religion, and Other Monsters

Jim Burgen

NELSON
BOOKS

An Imprint of Thomas Nelson

Published in Nashville, Tennessee, by Nelson Books, an imprint of Thomas Nelson. Nelson Books and Thomas Nelson are registered trademarks of HarperCollins Christian Publishing, Inc.

Thomas Nelson titles may be purchased in bulk for educational, business, fund-raising, or sales promotional use. For information, please e-mail SpecialMarkets@ ThomasNelson.com.

Unless otherwise indicated, Scripture quotations are taken from the Holy Bible, New International Version®. Copyright © 1973, 1978, 1984, 2011 by Biblica, Inc.™ Used by permission of Zondervan. All rights reserved worldwide. www.zondervan.com.

Italics added to Scripture quotations reflect the author's own emphasis.

Written and edited in association with Ben Foote.

Names and identifying details of some people mentioned in this book have been changed to protect their privacy.

Library of Congress Cataloging-in-Publication Data

Burgen, Jim, 1962–
  No more dragons : get free from broken dreams, lost hope, bad religion, and other monsters / Jim Burgen.
    pages cm
  Includes bibliographical references.
  ISBN 978-1-4002-0562-2
  1. Christian life. 2. Faith. 3. Anxiety—Religious aspects—Christianity. 4. Fear—Religious aspects—Christianity. I. Title.
  BV4501.3.B859 2014
  248.4—dc23   2013036354

Printed in the United States of America

HB 07.02.2018

To Robin, my wife, my best friend, and my hero.

CONTENTS

CONTENTS

1

YOU, ME, AND DRAGONS

What Is This Book About?

I've been staring at my computer screen for the last few days in an attempt to write the first line of whatever this thing is that I'm about to write. It's not off to a good start.

I could do something along the lines of a twelve-step program: *Hi, my name is Jim, and I'm a dragon.* Then everyone in the circle chimes, "Hi, Jim." But that feels weird and kind of depressing.

I could try the late-night infomercial route: *Attention! Are you tired of being a dragon? Call now and we'll send you our No More Dragons kit. But wait! There's more! If you call in the next thirty minutes, we'll throw in some steak knives!*

I'm sorry. This is simply how my brain works. I should

probably call my doctor and get my ADHD meds adjusted. (You think I'm kidding, but I'm not.)

As usual, I'm getting distracted.

Anyway, I guess I'll just start typing, and we'll see what comes out. I promise that somewhere along the way, I'll explain this "dragon" thing.

FROM PK TO DRAGON

I'll start with my story.

I'm a PK. That's a "preacher's kid" for all you normal people. I was born in Texas in a little town that had one flasher (a traffic light at an intersection, not a creepy guy with a trench coat). My dad, Chuck, was the pastor of a church in this tiny town, but we didn't stay there long. One of the elders told my dad he wasn't allowed to baptize an African American man in the church baptistery. He said to my dad, "Chuck, someday you'll understand that them Negroes don't have souls." I've even cleaned up that quote. My dad went home, told my mom to pack, and we left that town in our dust.

We spent the next several years in Oklahoma. I only have two real memories of our time there. Number one: We were at a rodeo when a bull got loose. Everybody had to run to the top of the fairground bleachers in order to escape sure death.

Number two: I choked on a lemon drop during one of my dad's Sunday morning sermons, and my gagging pretty much hijacked the service. When you're a PK, the congregation believes they have the right to parent you, so everybody took turns punching me in the back like a three-year-old piñata and yelling, "Breathe!" I guess the Heimlich maneuver hadn't made it to the panhandle of Oklahoma yet.

When I was five we moved to Indiana, where I lived until I headed off for college at eighteen. We lived in the parsonage of the church where my dad worked. This naturally meant three things. First, to most of the church members, our house was public property. No knocking, no privacy, and certainly no skipping church. Second, when it was nasty outside, I could roller-skate in the church basement. Third, in the summertime, when no one was looking, I was able to sneak a swim or two in the church baptistery. (My dad has gone to heaven, which makes that safe to confess now.)

I loved growing up in church. I loved all of it. Sunday morning church. Sunday school with the awesome felt-board Bible stories. Sunday night youth group, choir, Christmas Eve candlelight services, hay rides, summer camp. I did it all, and I loved every minute of it. (Except for once a year when *The Wizard of Oz* was on television on Sunday, and I was the only kid in the universe who wasn't able to watch it.) I still hold the award for Longest Army Crawl under the Pews Before Dad Catches You and Spanks You in Front of the Whole Church. (It's a long title for an award, but it was worth it.) When I was eight, my dad baptized me. Everything was cool. Life was good.

Until junior high. These three years between elementary school and high school are a merciless burden of pain and embarrassment in any boy's life. I don't think God makes mistakes, but if he did, junior high would be on the top of my list. Specifically, the whole puberty thing.

Maybe junior high is awesome if you're an early bloomer. I was not. I sang alto in the church choir until the eleventh grade. Without fail, every junior high physical education class assigned me a locker between Harry Bigfoot and Charlie Chest Hair.

Those were the years when my prayer life consisted of one prayer: *Dear God, I know you can do all things. I'm not asking for world peace, a cure for famine and disease, or protection from nuclear disaster. Instead, I have a simple request: one chest hair. Please. In Jesus' name, amen.*

The heavens were silent.

I could go on and on, but I won't. I'm just stressing that junior high was rough.

The worst part came from the most unexpected place: my church. For reasons that remain unknown, my church experienced a civil war that was anything but civil. My church blew to pieces.

To use church language, our congregation had a "split." A "split" is when one group of people becomes upset with another group of people about the direction a church is headed. The split usually occurs because of important stuff like the color of the carpet in the sanctuary or which brand of grape juice to use for Communion. So my church started fighting with one another, and somehow my dad was tossed into the crossfire of their religious turf war. In the name of "Christian sharing," they would spread vicious rumors about my family via pious prayer requests.

During that summer of my eighth grade year, as I watched my dad come home night after night, rest his head on the kitchen table, and cry as he felt the years of ministry slipping through his fingers, I learned a big lesson about Christianity: *Christians are mean.*

The truth is that only some Christians are mean, but at the time, I walked away thinking that *all* Christians were mean.

Christians can talk about love, sing about forgiveness, and quote Bible verses about grace, but when it comes to church politics, all that gets tossed out the window. Apparently, some Christians think they have found secret Bible verses that grant exception to the "Jesus and love" stuff when it comes to who gets to pick the worship songs and whether or not the choir will wear robes.

I watched helplessly as the church tore my dad to shreds—and then there was the straw that broke the camel's back. One evening, the elders called my dad into a last-minute church meeting in order to discuss an issue: "Chuck, we're concerned with how your wife, Ann, sits so rigidly at the organ when she plays for services. We think she looks arrogant. We need you to ask her to slouch a bit, so that she looks more humble when she's playing." For the record, at the age of thirteen, my mom had surgery to correct her scoliosis. The doctors fused her entire spine into one solid pillar, and after two years in a body cast, my mom couldn't slouch even if she wanted to.

When I heard the elders' complaint about my mom, I was done with Christians. You can punch me in the back like a three-year-old piñata. You can invade my house at your leisure. But when you use the semicamouflage of "Christian sharing" to assassinate my dad's character and criticize my mom, then I'm out.

I made a huge mistake during that season of my life. I assumed if Christians were that terrible, then Jesus was too. If the Christians who had been in my home, shared meals with me, done life with me, talked about their future with me, and made promises to me could suddenly change their minds and stab me in the back, break their promises, and attack everything I loved, then their leader, Jesus, was probably the same way.

I was done with Christians, but that doesn't mean I stopped going to church. No, that was not an option in our home. I still went to church every Sunday, but the other six days of the week were a very different story. One night during my freshman year of high school, I was invited to go to a Styx concert in Indianapolis. There, in Market Square Arena, some stranger offered me a funny-looking, hand-rolled cigarette and asked if I wanted a "hit."

I didn't think about it. I didn't pray about it. I didn't remember all those school lectures about the dangers of drugs or warnings that marijuana will turn you into a communist, or worse yet, a Democrat. Nope. I immediately said yes, took a toke, and (cue the Disney music) a whole new world opened up to me.

I don't use drugs anymore, and I don't believe that using any illegal drug is good or wise. But I'm going to be bluntly honest with you. Whoever said, "Drugs don't feel good" must have bought bad drugs, because I thought weed was awesome!

From that point on, I'd catch a buzz before, during, and after school. I started smoking pot before I even tried alcohol. I did eventually get around to having my first sip, and guess what? I liked that too! I wasn't fond of the cheap beer we stole from my buddy's grandpa's garage. Oh, no. I was into the good stuff. I'm talking about Boone's Farm Apple Wine with the screw-off top.

I soon discovered that you could get buzzed quicker with liquor. (Hey, that rhymed! I'm really hitting my stride with this whole writing thing.) When you're sixteen, you don't sip liquor from an expensive glass while you read poetry by a crackling fireplace. You chug as much as you can before the person next to you in the car pulls the bottle from your hands and takes his turn. Needless to say, the result is a quick buzz soon followed by a violent torrent of vomit in a stranger's front yard.

My entire high school career consisted of a few things: school plays, band, getting wasted on Saturday nights, and trying not to puke during church on Sundays.

Here is the crazy part: I felt no guilt. I felt no shame. I felt nothing. Not once did I think, *Hm, I wonder if this is a bit hypocritical or inconsistent with the words of Jesus.* Nope. The most stoned I've ever been in my entire life was on a church youth retreat. Everybody was inside the chapel singing "Pass It On," and I was in the woods with my buddies saying, "Pass it around."

College was more of the same. I attended a Christian liberal arts college in Tennessee. My choice of school had nothing to do with its connection to Christianity. My older sister went there, and when I visited her, I partied with her upperclassman boyfriend and his buddies. My decision to attend that college came down to three basic criteria. One, I had already made some friends there. Two, it was five hundred miles from my home. Three, the legal drinking age in Tennessee at the time was nineteen. *Sign me up! Hail to thee, our alma mater . . .*

I was premed my freshman year because I wanted to be a dentist. Why? Simple. My orthodontist was rich, and he drove a Porsche. My family was poor. We lived in a dumpy house that belonged to a church, and we drove a used car with wood paneling down the side.

The dentist dream didn't last long. It turns out that to be in the dental profession, you need to excel at subjects like chemistry. By the end of my freshman year, I was on academic probation. During my brief studies in dentistry, I also discovered my deep aversion to human spit and bad breath. Nobody went to the dentist to inform the good doctor that everything was sparkling white and spiffy. Instead, they went because of plaque, halitosis, and refusal to deny themselves sweets. I learned it wasn't uncommon for people to finally break down and go to the dentist because something was about to explode, rupture, or disintegrate, and their mouths smelled like a dinosaur dumped between their back molars. (I'm dry heaving just thinking about it.)

Between the local bar's dollar pitcher nights, my

inadequate studies of molecular compounds, and the depraved condition of the human mouth, I let go of my dream to be a dentist.

Skip ahead to sophomore year. I was at swim practice when I ran into someone. I stood up, and there she was. Robin Carter. A junior.

She said, "Hi!"

I said, "Hi!"

She asked, "Do you want to play sea otter?"

I didn't know what she meant, but just like Market Square Arena, I didn't think or pray about it. Without hesitation, I replied, "Why, yes I do," and for the next hour or so, we played "sea otter." It's pretty hard to explain "sea otter." Basically, it's a game where you swim around without the use of your arms and act like a sea otter. Hey, there you have it! I guess it's not hard to explain after all.

After sea otter, I walked her to the dining hall and asked if she would go out with me Saturday night. She said she would. That night, I went to a Foreigner/Billy Squier concert and smoked my last joint. The next night, I went on my first date with Robin, and that's when everything started to change.

She didn't disclose this fact during our sea ottering, but Robin was a Christian. A real one. On our first date she asked if I would go to church with her the next morning.

"Sure, I'd love to," is what came out of my mouth.

Noooo! is what rumbled on the inside. I had moved to Tennessee in order to escape church. But the logic was unavoidable: *I like Robin. Robin likes church. To be with Robin, I need to go to church.* So I started going back to church.

I'm sure it's different now, but at the time, church in East Tennessee was—what's the word?—horrible. Imagine Jesus meets the movie *Deliverance*. It was like someone had pushed the wrong button on a time machine, and we'd all gone back to the pioneer days. Everybody in church had the same last name. I swear, I was waiting for someone to approach me and say, "Hey, y'all! We're the Clampetts. A hundred years ago, our grandpappies were traveling west and got stuck here. We stayed ever since. Anyway, welcome to church."

After some church hopping, Robin and I settled in at a campus student ministry at the nearby East Tennessee State University. Unlike the other churches we'd tried, this one seemed okay. We met in an empty classroom, there was no dress code, and a few students led worship songs with lyrics that were taken straight from the Bible in a way that made sense and sounded great.

The preacher's name was Tommy. At first, I had my doubts. I fully expected the flannel-shirted, scraggly bearded, hillbilly preacher to tell us we were all pieces of crap, but because Jesus was so nice, he might cut us a break if we apologized enough times. But that never happened. Tommy would tell these great stories about mountains or ducks or planets or cars, and then, when he had you totally captivated, he would say something like, "You see, it's the same way with Jesus." And you would sit there and think, *I've read that Bible story all my life, but I've never thought about it like that.*

One Sunday, Robin and I showed up late, and we were forced to sit dead center in the front row. Just as I began thumbing through the Old Testament for anything remotely violent or sexual to chuckle at, Tommy took the stage and began telling a story from *The Voyage of the Dawn Treader* in The Chronicles of Narnia by C. S. Lewis.

FROM DRAGON TO BOY

The story takes place in a magical world called Narnia, and it's about a boy named Eustace and a few of his friends. Eustace is arrogant, selfish, unfriendly, and generally disliked by almost every other character in the story. During their travels throughout the vast world of Narnia, the children run the ship ashore on a mysterious island. Eustace wanders off by himself and ends up stumbling upon a cave containing a dragon's hoard of treasure.

Eustace, who is a greedy kid, realizes he could be as rich as a king in Narnia if he keeps the treasure for himself. Exhausted from the excitement of discovering the dragon's riches, Eustace falls asleep on top of the towering stack of crowns, jewels, and gold coins. When Eustace wakes up the next morning, he has been transformed into a dragon. He sees his reflection in a lake and realizes he is nothing but a monster: "Sleeping on a dragon's hoard with greedy, dragonish thoughts in his heart, he had become a dragon himself."[1] In Narnia, if you think dragon thoughts and do dragon things, eventually you will become a dragon.

Eustace is no longer a chubby little boy. He is a monster. He isn't who he used to be. He isn't who he wants to be. He's not who he was created and designed to be. The only friends he has are now terrified of him. Eustace is a dragon.

I was sitting on the edge of my front-row seat in a university classroom, listening to a country preacher tell a story about a boy in an imaginary world who turned into a mythical dragon, and my chest started to feel tight. My heart started to beat faster. I had tears in my eyes. He was telling my story. This story was about me.

Becoming a dragon is a dangerously sneaky process. Becoming a dragon takes a long string of bad choices and decisions you don't even realize you're making until it's too late. One day you glance at yourself in the mirror, and a monster is staring back at you. You think back on your life, add up your countless mistakes, and realize you aren't who you used to be. You aren't who you want to be. You're not who you were created and designed to be. Instead, you're a dragon.

As I sat in that classroom in East Tennessee, I came to a realization: it was not difficult to screw up my life. But how would I ever unscrew it? The nineteen-year-old boy in Tennessee had the same problem as the little boy in Narnia: I knew I didn't want to be a dragon anymore, but I didn't know how to stop.

Back to the Narnia story. Eustace sadly walks into the forest. He is alone, confused, and defeated. He has resigned himself to the fact that he will always be a dragon and there is no hope for change. This is precisely when he meets Aslan, the talking lion. For those of you who are not familiar with C. S. Lewis's Chronicles of Narnia, Aslan represents Jesus in these stories.

Aslan looks Eustace in the eyes and beckons to him. Fearful yet strangely compelled, Eustace follows the huge lion to a mountaintop garden. Standing by a well of clear water, Aslan instructs the boy-turned-dragon to undress.

At first Eustace is confused, because he isn't wearing any clothes. But then he remembers that he's a giant lizard, and all reptiles can shed their skin. So Eustace tries to free himself. He painfully tears away at his layer of scales, but underneath is another layer. He begins ripping into the new layer, but underneath is yet another layer. He continues to repeat this process until he is absolutely exhausted from the pain. He simply can't do it anymore and whimpers to Aslan in defeat.

Aslan replies, "You will have to let me undress you."[2]

Back in Tennessee, I had ceased breathing ten minutes prior. I was more aware than ever that the story was not about a little boy in a fantasy world called Narnia. The story was, without a doubt, written about me. I didn't want to be a dragon anymore, but I couldn't fix myself. I needed to have Jesus do it for me.

In the story, Eustace reluctantly and fearfully agrees to let Aslan shed his scales. He lies down on his dragon back, and Aslan plunges his enormous claws into Eustace's chest. The pain is unbearable. Finally, the lion reaches deep into the chest cavity of the dragon and pulls out a small, trembling boy who is dripping with filth.

Aslan then throws Eustace's pale body into the waters of the well, and in a few moments, Eustace breaks the surface of the water and gasps for air. He is no longer a dragon. He is finally the boy he was created to be. He is washed, clean, changed, and made whole. His friends are no longer scared of him. In fact, when his friend Edmund sees Eustace, he exclaims, "You have been—well, un-dragoned."[3]

When Tommy finished telling the story, I had tears streaming down my face. I needed to be washed, cleaned, changed, and made whole. And I knew there was only one person who could do that for me. I then uttered the prayer that changed my entire life: *Dear Father, if you can undragon me, you can have my whole life.*

I wish I could say I never again did anything that dragons do, but that's not true. I can tell you that my life gradually began to change after I bumped into Jesus in that classroom in East Tennessee. God changed me through a story written by a dead English theologian about a fantasy world where little boys can become dragons and then, with the help of a giant lion, become little boys again.

As Jesus started to strip the scales from my back, I began wanting different things for my life. I started thinking about different stuff. I wanted to learn more about the loving, gracious, holy yet approachable God and his Son who came to earth. I desired to know this Jesus, who wanted to tell me he loved me despite the things I had done instead of lecture me about what a disappointment I was. I finally saw that, in spite of the long list of reasons God could hate me, he didn't. He not only loved me, but he wanted us to live together—me with him and him with me. He wanted to change my life, not just after my funeral in some far-off place called heaven, but right then and there and every moment after.

God had been tapping on my shoulder for quite some

time. *Hey, Jim. Hey, Jim. Hey, Jim!* My reply to his faint call had consistently been, "Go away!" But on that day in Tennessee, God didn't tap me on the shoulder. He hit me over the side of the head with a two-by-four and shouted, *Jim, will you just talk to me?*

"What? What do you want?"

I want you. I want all of you.

Looking back over those years, I can see that his voice was always there. He was always whispering to me. Always pursuing me. All he ever wanted me to do was talk with him, but my consistent attitude was, "Yeah, right! I know how that conversation will go. It will start with how disappointed you are in me. You'll follow that with a few 'you should have known betters' and 'how could you be so stupids?' Then, at some point, you will hit the big, red 'Go directly to hell' button, and I'm firewood for eternity. No thanks. I'm not interested in that conversation."

I tried to keep my head down, barrel through, and pretend that everything was fine. That's the same as standing in the middle of the railroad tracks and chanting loudly over the sound of the approaching horn, "There is no train, there is no train, there is no train!"

There *is* a train. And if you pretend there isn't, it will eventually flatten you.

From that point on, God and I began to talk more. I brought up my sins and my mistakes. He didn't. I gave him my laundry list of failures, fears, insecurity-driven lies, and poor choices. He didn't. He didn't throw one thing in my face. I mattered so much to him, and my past sins didn't. He had forgiven them.

My hunger to know God more, my failing grades in chemistry, and my disgust for anything tooth related prompted me to change my major to biblical studies and sociology. Studying God and studying people seemed like a good combination. It also led to a wrestling match with God.

It happened in a parking lot behind Robin's dorm the beginning of my junior year. The *Hey, Jim!* tapping on the shoulder had graduated into a loud but distinct voice saying, *Hey, Jim! I want you to be a pastor.*

Of course, my prayerful response was, *Dear heavenly Father, no. In Jesus' name, amen.*

There was no way I was going to become a pastor! I had seen the church thing. I had met some of "God's people," and (no offense) they were the biggest collection of weirdoes and turds ever assembled. They spoke in their own language, one that wasn't about anything real or helpful. They referred to Jesus, but usually only to manipulate people into doing stuff they didn't want to do.

"No way, God! I've been there. I've seen it. I bought the T-shirt, and I'm never going back. I was run over by your church, and I'm not going to let it happen again. Find someone else." The shouting match lasted several hours that night until I finally struck up a deal with God on a curb in the parking lot. (I'm not sure if you're allowed to do that, but I did, and I wasn't struck by lightning.)

The deal went something like this: "Okay, God. I'll do it . . . on one condition. I'll do it as long as you let me talk about real stuff. I want to talk about real problems and real life in real ways to real people. If I'm allowed to be real and talk about the stuff that nobody ever talked to me about, then I'll do it. Do we have a deal?"

The heavens were silent.

There was no giant beam of light splitting the sky. There was no thundering voice rolling over the campus. There was no supernatural, floating hand scribbling messages on the asphalt. But the peace that followed that conversation might as well have been a bullhorn straight from the throne of God himself saying, *Talk about real issues in a real way? That's all I ever wanted from you anyway.*

NO MORE DRAGONS

That is the origin of my thirty-year-and-counting journey of church and ministry and marriage and parenting and truth and grace and success and failure and "what was I thinking?" moments and "aha!" moments. As Jesus said,

> The thief comes only to steal and kill and destroy; I
> have come that they may have life, and have it to the
> full. (John 10:10)

My "life to the full" began the moment God started claw-ing away my scales.

I've spent the last three decades trying to figure out which things will steal, kill, and destroy my life and which things will make it better. I'm sure that the remaining decades (or minutes) between now and my funeral will be more of the same struggle.

This is your journey, too, isn't it? Before us are count-less choices. We struggle to discern which ones will lead us to better lives and which ones will kill us, which ones add scales to our dragons and which ones slough them off. We have to learn which path will make us the people God wants us to be and which path will awaken the dragon.

Here are some daunting questions: If you're already a dragon, is it possible to be un-dragoned? Is it possible to have your scales removed? Is it possible to become the person God intended when he said, "Let there be you"?

Jesus said that with God all things are possible (Matthew 19:26), which must include the miracle of being rescued from your scaly exterior. Everything that fol-lows in this book revolves around that theme. It is the theme of impossible things becoming reality. It is the theme of escaping our broken dreams, restoring our lost hope, ignoring bad religion, and erasing the distorted definitions we've given ourselves. It is the theme of Jesus un-dragoning our lives.

Before you turn another page, let me say this: Some of you reading this may be saying, "I'm already a Christian. I'm just reading this book because I have a friend . . . blah, blah, blah." Okay, whatever. If you think God has already rescued you from your dragons, I have no delusion that you will agree with everything that follows in this book. I've wrestled through its content with close, faithful friends, and I happen to believe that I'm more right than wrong. But then again, I used to think that Boone's Farm Apple Wine was the good stuff. So sift through the rest of this book and make your own decisions. Compare it to what God says in his Word. Keep the good, and trash the bad. That's biblical (1 Thessalonians 5:21–22).

Here is my hope. If you read this book, disagree with some of what I've said, and discuss it with some people, then at least you'll be wrestling through stuff that matters and not "important" stuff like what people should wear to church and who gets to take home the poinsettias after the Christmas Eve service. Let's wrestle through some tougher issues like:

- Is Jesus the only one who can un-dragon people?
- What was the most frequently asked question of Jesus in the gospels, and what was his response?
- How do you follow Jesus?
- What is faith and how does it work?
- What happens if you didn't mean to become a dragon?
- Where is God in difficult times?
- Why don't you and I like most churches?
- What did God say a healthy church is supposed to look like?
- What does God ask of his followers when partnering with him in the redemptive, restorative, reconciling message and ministry of Jesus Christ?

I'm not the Holy Spirit (cue the "Hallelujah Chorus"), and I don't always get it right; but if you ask the Holy Spirit to teach you something from the pages of this book, he'll show up. In fact, I wouldn't be surprised if he's been tapping on your shoulder too.

I've spent the last thirty years trying to find the answers to these questions. This book is where I've landed.

This whole first chapter has been one long story building up to the shortest recovery group introduction you've ever read:

Hi, my name is Jim. I was a boy. I became a dragon. Jesus made me a boy again. He rescued me from being a dragon and gave me a second chance. And I know he wants to do the same for you. He wants you to have a life with no more lies, guilt, shame, or condemnation. A life with no more dragons.

2

MONKEYS, NAKED PEOPLE, AND TRAITORS

Only Jesus Slays Your Dragons

I grew up in a church that taught the Bible. I went to camps and conferences that taught the Bible. I attended a college that drew its founding principles from the Bible. However, it wasn't the Bible that got my attention. It was a hillbilly preacher's ability to connect the truth of the Bible with what was going on in my life. He taught in a way that enabled me to realize, "Hey, that's kind of like my life. I've felt like that before. Maybe this Jesus thing could work for me." The Bible didn't get my attention; Tommy's story-telling did.

Before you write me off as "Bible light" or think I put

more stock into some country preacher than I do into Scripture's "thus sayeth the Lords," just take a breath. In all of history, the best country-preacher-slash-storyteller ever to connect biblical truths to the realities of his audience's everyday lives was Jesus himself.

Jesus taught ancient truths in ways that made them seem completely fresh. He adapted his stories to his crowds. He did this with farmers, shepherds, fishermen, financial investors, soldiers, parents, hookers, IRS agents, construction workers, doctors, and used camel salesmen. (All right, I made up that last one.) Whenever Jesus would finish telling a story, people in the crowd would say, "Dang! This carpenter-turned-preacher guy makes sense! I've never heard anything like it!"

When it comes to God's truth, Jesus didn't change a single stroke of the pen (Matthew 5:17–18). When people heard Jesus teach and thought, *I've never heard anything like this*, they had. It was written all over the Old Testament. They just hadn't ever heard someone make it so relatable before. That was Jesus' specialty.

Jesus knew that the best way for people to connect the dots between God's truth and their lives was to tell a great story. Why would we imagine it to be any different today? With that being said, let's tackle a new story and a few old stories that will refresh the timeless fact that only Jesus has the power to un-dragon our lives.

MONKEYS

Before I moved to Colorado, I lived in Nicholasville, Kentucky, a small town outside of Lexington. Kentucky, as I'm sure you know, is famous for several things: college basketball (go Cats!), horse racing, bourbon, tobacco, moonshine, and of course, fried chicken.

It gets better. The "Happy Birthday" song comes from Kentucky. Also, Kentucky is known for nearly two gazillion casserole dishes that incorporate Campbell's condensed soup and Velveeta. And there's the gravy. I don't know if Kentuckians invented gravy, but they certainly put it on everything.

There is one other thing that Kentucky is famous for (well, at least to me), and that is the Primate Rescue Center located just a few miles from my old house in Nicholasville. The Primate Rescue Center is exactly what the name implies. It's a center that rescues and rehabilitates monkeys and other primates that are no longer wanted or adequately cared for.

Believe it or not, there was once a time when, in certain states, you could pick up the phone and order yourself a monkey. How cool does that sound? Answer: *very* cool.

I did some research and learned that for a small, plain ol' brown monkey, you only had to drop a few hundred dollars. But if you were willing to spend ten, twenty, sometimes even thirty thousand dollars, you could own your very own chimpanzee.

Again, this sounds *very* cool. Let's be honest, owning a monkey or a chimpanzee for a pet would be so much fun. Slap a pair of jeans, a T-shirt, and a ball cap on a chimpanzee, and he starts to look like a tiny, hairy man. The two of you could spend all day together. He could teach you how to peel bananas, and you could teach him how to play video games and wash your car. Life would be perfect, right?

Wrong. Monkeys and chimps are wild animals, so they are going to do wild things. One day, you're going to hold Hairy Larry (that's what I'd name my monkey) up to your face like you've done a hundred times before, and you're going to say something like, "Who's my little cutie-patootie?" But this time, your cutie-patootie will throw crap at you (literally) or he'll bite your face off because Hairy Larry is *not* cutie or patootie. He's a wild animal trapped in a place he was never meant to be.

The question I want to get to is not, "How do you get a monkey?" but, "How do you get rid of a monkey you don't want anymore?" As I learned, you call the Primate Rescue Center, and they'll pick up Hairy Larry and drive him back to Kentucky.

One day, in my veterinarian's office, I saw a notice posted on the bulletin board that announced the Primate Rescue Center's annual open house day. Back then the

Primate Rescue Center was only open to the public one day a year. On their open house day, the public was invited to tour the facility and hopefully make a donation to fund the other 364 days of the year. Being an animal and outdoors kind of guy, I didn't want to miss it, so I marked it on my calendar and showed up bright and early on open house day in order to see what went on behind those mysterious gates.

The Center was a series of buildings, extensions, and cages where the rescued primates were housed and treated. In front of each cage was a large sign that explained what type of primate it contained as well as the story of how that animal made its home at the Center.

As I made the rounds, I came to a cage that contained a very fat monkey who was lazing on a ledge. He didn't move. His eyes were half-closed. I'm pretty sure I heard him burp a couple of times, and I think he scratched himself inappropriately. He sort of reminded me of myself when I watch football on Sunday afternoons.

He made me laugh, so I read his story. He used to live as someone's pet in an apartment in Chicago, but he had bitten his owner several times. The owner's solution to this problem was to have all his teeth pulled. While this kept the monkey from biting, it also rendered him incapable of eating. When the monkey grew weaker and weaker from starvation, his jerk owner decided simply to open the apartment window and toss the dying animal onto the snowy fire escape. Owner's problem: solved. Monkey's problem: much worse.

Luckily, a neighbor saw the whole thing and called the Humane Society, who rescued the monkey from certain death. The Primate Rescue Center took over from there, and after months of rehabilitation and plenty of TLC, the once-emaciated monkey was now fat and healthy. Notice that I didn't say happy. You could tell. You could see it in his eyes. He was sad. He was just a sad, fat monkey.

After reading his story, I was very interested in the other primates' stories. Next to the sad, fat monkey was an insane monkey with a Mohawk. No joke. He was rocking back and forth on a stool, and he had crazy eyes that darted back and forth. Every once in a while, he would unleash a piercing scream, bolt around the cage, and then return to rocking on his stool and looking around the room with his beady eyes.

There are labs in America that test products and medical procedures on monkeys to make sure they are safe before trying them on human beings. In this monkey's case, a medical lab decided to find out how much of a particular illegal street drug a living creature could ingest before completely frying his brain. At the expense of this monkey, they found out. When they were finished with their tests, they called the Primate Rescue Center and said, "Hey, we're done with this monkey. But now he's brain-dead and addicted to drugs. Come take him off our hands."

The open house tour went on for quite a while. Finally, we came to the main attraction of the Center: a large outdoor habitat where they kept the chimpanzees. There must have been ten or twelve of them in a cage the size of a two-story house. Inside, the staff had placed playground equipment to climb on, ropes and tires to swing on, and hay bales for bedding and giant pillow fights. As I walked up to the cage, a young chimpanzee sneaked up on a grandpa chimpanzee and hit him over the head with a hay bale. The youngster screamed with joy, and the old guy just looked annoyed. In fact, I think I heard him mumble some chimpanzee expletives. But overall, they seemed content, peaceful, and safe. They hadn't always been that way though.

Several years earlier, an elderly woman in Georgia kept five of these adult chimpanzees, whom she called her "babies," confined in a 10'x10' metal cell inside a concrete building. No light. No windows. The doors of the cage became corroded shut, and when the rescuers arrived, they were horrified to discover more than four feet of feces that the intelligent chimps had pushed to the side to give themselves just enough room in which to live. The rescuers learned that the chimps had rarely received food or water, and they had never received medical care. They had not been outside their 10'x10' prison cell in more than twenty years.

Shortly after the chimps were rescued, one of the five died. After months of medical treatments and rehabilitation, the other four found a safe home at the Primate Rescue Center. I guess that's good news, but, as I stood watching those poor, neglected, lost, and broken creatures, a voice inside me was screaming, *This isn't the way it was supposed to be!*

I don't know precisely how all of creation happened, but I can't imagine that when God created the chimpanzee, he paused, scratched his bearded chin, and exclaimed, "I know what would be perfect for these little guys! How about a 10'x10' metal box with no light, no air, but plenty of waste and filth? Yep. Let's go with that."

No way! It was more like, "I know what would be perfect for these little guys! How about a jungle with vines, trees, running streams, and other chimpanzees they can play with, swing around with, and eat bananas with? Yep. They're going to love that."

In the case of those chimps at the Primate Rescue Center, they probably *would* have loved that lifestyle, but they never got the chance. With those chimps, something went wrong. Someone was supposed to take care of them but had neglected them. Someone was supposed to protect them but had hurt them.

Maybe, somewhere along the way, those monkeys had bad days and made bad decisions, like biting their owners.

Or maybe they were the victims of someone else's bad decisions, like being test subjects for drug use. Either way, it didn't matter anymore *how* they hit rock-bottom; the only thing that mattered was that they were there.

If the staff of the Primate Rescue Center hadn't paid attention, listened to their cries, left their homes, and come looking for them to set them free, even at their own great risk, then those chimps would have died inside suffocating traps.

You're smart, so you see what I'm up to. We're not talking about monkeys in Kentucky anymore.

We're talking about us.

We're talking about Jesus.

NAKED PEOPLE

As you read through the biographies of Jesus, you repeatedly find Jesus leaving his home and searching for people who weren't living the lives they were created to live. Every time he bumped into these people, Jesus looked at them and said something to the effect of, "This isn't what you were meant for. There's a better way to live your life. Follow me, and I'll take you there."

I'll give you a few of my favorite examples.

One day, Jesus was walking through a town when a mob of men threw a naked girl at his feet (John 8:1–11).

These men had caught this girl having sex with a man she wasn't married to, and one of the mob leaders asked Jesus, "Hey, Teacher. We caught this girl in the act of sinning. She's guilty, and there's no doubt about it. Moses gave us a law that says sinners like her deserve to be stoned to death. What do you say? Do you agree or disagree?"

This was a trick question. If Jesus replied, "Don't stone her," then the mob would say that Jesus was also a sinner because he refused to obey God's laws. If Jesus replied, "Stone her," then the mob would say that he was mean, heartless, and intolerant. They thought they had Jesus trapped—but of course, Jesus was smarter.

Jesus didn't immediately say anything. Instead, he knelt down and scribbled in the dust for a few moments before he finally stood up and replied, "You're right. The law says that all sinners deserve to be condemned and punished. In this case, they should be stoned. So how about this? If you've never sinned, you can go first. You can throw the first stone. Then the rest of us will jump in, and we'll give this girl what she deserves."

Obviously, I wasn't there, but I'm guessing it got quiet and awkward for a few minutes as the mob mulled over Jesus' words. Jesus implied a terrifying truth in that statement: "All sinners deserve to be condemned. So if you want, we can start with her and work our way through the crowd passing out judgment and punishment until only the perfect people are left. If those are the rules you want to play by, then fine. When I count to three and blow this whistle, anyone who has never sinned can go to town on the sinners."

If they played by those rules, Jesus would have been the last one standing. So the mob dropped their stones and went home, and Jesus was left alone in the street with the terrified, naked girl.

Now, if I were that girl, I would be thinking, *This is the worst day of my life.* I'd probably still have my eyes shut tight, waiting for that first stone to make contact. I'd hope it would go by fast. I'd hope someone could put me out of my misery.

How do you think that girl wound up in that situation? What led her to that place? I'm guessing that when she was in middle school, she didn't write in her yearbook, "I hope that someday I'm caught in a hotel sleeping with some married guy who will never leave his wife like he promised. I hope a mob kicks down the door and drags me to the alley so I can lay naked and ashamed while they have a meeting about how to kill me. That's the life I'm aiming for."

That wasn't what she had hoped for. But it didn't matter anymore *how* she hit rock-bottom; it only mattered that she was there.

What did Jesus do? He rescued her. He reached into

her mess, picked her up from the dirt, covered up her nakedness and shame, and told her, "This isn't what you were meant for. Things have to change. There's a better way to live life. Follow me, and I'll take you there."

Jesus was the only person in the entire crowd who was qualified to throw the first stone of condemnation. He was the only person without sin. He had every right to look that girl in the face and say, "I'll do it. It's time to get what you deserve." But instead of giving her what she deserved, Jesus gave her what she needed. Jesus paid attention, heard her cries, left his home, risked his safety for her sake, set her free, and pointed her toward the life she was created to live. Only Jesus could have stoned her. And only Jesus could tear her out of the dragon.

TRAITORS

Another time, as Jesus was walking down a road, he looked up in a tree and saw a short guy named Zacchaeus (Luke 19:1–9). Zacchaeus, a Jew from Jericho, had taken a job collecting taxes for the occupying Roman military. The closest comparison I can come up with is a guy from New York City, a few days after 9/11, charging people to look at the wreckage of the Twin Towers, pocketing a portion of that toll, and then sending the rest to finance further al-Qaeda attacks.

That is what Zacchaeus was all about. He was an Israelite profiting off the invading Roman government. He stole money from his fellow Jews who were already hurting, gave some to Caesar, and stuck some in an offshore bank account. He got rich by exploiting his own. He joined the enemy. He was a traitor.

Needless to say, Zacchaeus wasn't too popular.

So one day, Zacchaeus climbed a tree in order to get a good look at this famous storyteller he had heard so much about. Jesus stopped under the tree, looked up, and said, "Zacchaeus, come down. Let's go have lunch at your place."

That did not go over well with the locals. During lunch, there were emergency meetings being held and last-minute text-messages being sent: "Jesus, why do you keep hanging out with sinners?"

In fact, the number one question asked of Jesus in the Bible was not, "Who is God?" "How do I get to heaven?" or "What is the meaning and purpose of my life?" Those are all great questions, but that's not what people asked him. Instead, the most frequently asked question of Jesus that I find in the Bible is some variation of, "Why do you hang out, eat lunch, and become friends with sinners?"

Jesus always replied, "These are the people I love. I left my home for these people. I came to seek and save that which is lost."

How do you think Zacchaeus felt? He couldn't even have someone over for lunch without the entire town being shocked. How do you think he wound up in that situation? I'm pretty sure that back when he was a kid, he didn't scribble in his journal, "I hope I grow up to become a traitor. I hope I walk away from my faith, family, friends, and people in order to work for the Romans. I hope everybody hates me. That's the life I'm aiming for."

The Bible doesn't tell us how he wound up a traitor, but if he was anything like you and me, Zacchaeus had his dragons. Maybe he got tired of the "short guy" jokes that other people thought were so funny. Maybe each joke killed a part of his soul.

Or maybe people kept telling Zacchaeus that he didn't fit in, and after hearing it enough times, he believed it. That's what happened to my friend Bob. One day, he confessed to me that he was gay. In his own words, "My older brother used to hold me down and molest me when I was a kid. All my life, people have called me names like 'sissy,' 'faggot,' and 'queer.' That's how people see me. That's what people think and say about me. I guess that's what I am."

Maybe that's what Zacchaeus was going through: "My family doesn't want me. My friends make fun of me. My religious community doesn't think I'm good enough to be around. Fine. I'm out. I'll take my ball and go home."

Zacchaeus wasn't living the life he had always hoped

for. But, again, it didn't matter *how* he hit rock-bottom; it only mattered that he was there. When Zacchaeus and his towering baggage bumped into Jesus, how did Jesus respond? "Hey, Zacchaeus. Let's be friends. Do you want to have lunch?"

The curious thing about this story is that Jesus and Zacchaeus ate lunch, but before dessert was served, Zacchaeus stood up and announced to everyone within shouting distance, "Look, Lord! Here and now I give half of my possessions to the poor, and if I have cheated anybody out of anything, I will pay back four times the amount" (Luke 19:8).

I wonder what transpired over lunch, what part of the conversation caused such a shift in Zacchaeus. Maybe Jesus said something like, "Zacchaeus, I get it. I understand what's going on in your life. I understand how you got here, but this isn't the life I meant for you. You weren't created for this. You've made a mess that has dominated your life, but it doesn't have to anymore. There's a better way to live. Follow me, and I'll take you there."

Instead of giving Zacchaeus what he deserved, Jesus gave him what he needed. Jesus paid attention, left his home, ate lunch with him at the risk of his own safety, set him free, and pointed Zacchaeus toward the life he was meant to live. Jesus ripped Zacchaeus free from the dragon.

EVEN MORE NAKED PEOPLE

Another time, as soon as Jesus hopped out of his boat, a naked dude came tearing down the beach, foaming at the mouth (Mark 5:1–20). The naked guy fell on the ground in front of Jesus and started screaming, "What do you want with me, Jesus?" (v. 7).

This naked guy had been involved with evil spirits, and the spirits had decided to set up shop inside his soul. This guy used to have a normal life, but now he ran around screaming and possessed. Occasionally, someone would catch him and try to fix him, but he always managed to break loose and run back to his old life. He ended up living in a cemetery. During the night, he would take sharp rocks and cut himself. His cries would roll past the tombs and frighten people in the nearby towns.

So Jesus hopped out of his boat and bumped into a bloody, screaming, cursing, naked guy who essentially whimpered, "Jesus, what do you want with me? I know who you are and what you must think of me. Swear to God you won't hurt me. Please leave me alone."

Jesus loved this guy, so he opted not to leave him alone. Instead, he sent away the evil spirits that had infested the man for far too long. Then Jesus and the guy sat down on a rock, struck up a conversation, and by the time the townspeople showed up, he was clothed and in his right mind for the first time in years.

Once again, we don't know how the conversation went, but based on the character of Jesus that we see elsewhere, Jesus didn't lecture the man about the dangers of demons. The man knew well the dangers of demons. Jesus didn't tell the man that it was harmful to cut himself. I doubt Jesus told him to stop acting like a crazy person. That would have been pointless because crazy people typically have no choice but to act crazy.

Maybe Jesus simply answered the man's question. Maybe Jesus sat down with the man and said, "You want to know what I want *from* you? Here's your answer: nothing. Instead, I want something better *for* you. You're afraid I'm going to torture, harm, or punish you for what you've done. I'm not. I'd rather heal you, forgive you, and help you live a better life. You're afraid I'm mad at you for the mess you've made of your life. I'm not. I don't hate you. I love you.

"You're the reason I left heaven and came down here. I came looking for you so that we could have this moment right here, right now, on this beach. I came to set you free from your dragon. Now go home to your family, tell everybody what God has done for you, and enjoy your new life."

JESUS SLAYS DRAGONS

Isn't it odd how we often find ourselves making choices that, only a few years, months, or days ago, we never would have imagined possible? We wake up one day and everything is different. We open our eyes and realize we're nothing like the people we hoped we'd become, and we're living lives we were never intended to live. It's a terrible "aha" moment.

What happened? When did everything change? When did everything go so wrong?

Maybe your story is similar to that of the naked girl thrown at Jesus' feet. You thought you were in love. You believed the promises of a person who swore up and down that he loved you and would stay with you forever. But he didn't. He lied, used you up, and left. You lost hope and began a long string of poor choices, decisions, and relationships. It wouldn't surprise you, if you were thrown at the feet of Jesus, to be stoned with condemnation and punishment for your mistakes.

Or maybe your story is like Zacchaeus's. When you were young, you believed God was good and people were kind, but eventually you discovered that people were mean, cruel, and evil. Somebody held you down, hurt you, and took something precious from you. Certain people made you feel like you were nothing but a rag to wipe up their own filth.

On top of all of this, it felt like God didn't care and wouldn't help. So you gave up on God, people, and yourself. You worked hard, played hard, and did whatever was necessary in order to get ahead. You used and abused people, and you ended up becoming the kind of person who had mistreated you in the past. Now you look behind you and see nothing but a long trail of wounded, angry victims. You might be curious about Jesus, but you're not brave enough to have a conversation with him because you think it wouldn't go well. You're hiding up in the tree.

Or maybe your story is similar to that of the naked guy on the beach. Your life is suffocated by darkness, pain, depression, oppression, and hopelessness. You're already as good as dead. Your home is a cemetery. At night, you wail, "God, what do you want from me? What have I done? Why is this happening? Why won't it stop? Please just let me die!"

I don't know your story. Maybe it's completely different from all of the above examples. I assure you that Jesus' response to your story will stay the same. Not once do you ever find Jesus bumping into messy people and then bashing them over the head with condemnation, judgment, and anger. He never lectures them about their many mistakes or reminds them of how far they've fallen short.

In all my years of going to church, never once have I walked through the front doors thinking, *Boy, I hope the preacher reminds me of all the ways I've screwed up my life so far. That's why I got out of bed. I came to church this morning for a good, heaping dose of guilt and condemnation.*

I've never needed that. I'm already very aware of my guilt and warranted condemnation. I don't need reminding. I'm looking for the same thing the naked girl, the naked guy, and Zacchaeus were all looking for: something better. Something freer.

I'm looking for someone to set me free from my 10'x10' prison cell before it becomes my tomb. I need to know there's hope. I need to know I still have a chance. I need someone to slay my dragons.

Jesus understands this, so he meets you wherever you are. Whether you're lying in the street, naked and humiliated; or you're hiding in the trees, hated and empty; or you're living in a cemetery, covered in the bloody scars from self-inflicted wounds, Jesus wants you to bump into him. And every time, Jesus will offer the same hope:

> The thief comes only to steal and kill and destroy; I have come that they may have life, and have it to the full. (John 10:10)

In other words, to quote the great theologians Led Zeppelin, from their masterpiece "Stairway to Heaven":

There's still time to change the road you're on.[1]

There is a path in life that will rip you off, kill everyone and everything that's important to you, and leave nothing but destruction and devastation in its wake. If you choose that path, you will become a dragon and stay one.

But there's another path in life that is full and abundant. This path leads to the life you were designed and created to live. Jesus heard your cries, left his home, sacrificed his life, and conquered death so that you could have a shot at this better life.

Other people may have given up on you. You may have given up on yourself.

But Jesus has not given up on you.

Through Jesus, and only Jesus, you can be un-dragoned. You can be free again. You can have hope, joy, and a full life. The question is not whether this whole thing is truth or fairy tale. It's absolute truth. The question is whether or not you're going to stand up from the dusty ground, get down out of that tree, or leave the cemetery behind.

3

YOUR PAST, YOUR PRESENT, AND YOUR TRAIN TRACKS

Believing Without Aligning Is Useless

The easy, feel-good, refreshing truth from the previous chapter is that Jesus doesn't hate you and he's not mad at you. He loves you, and he wants to tear apart the messes you've made and pull you from the belly of the dragon. Believing that Jesus is willing and capable to free you from your oppressive monsters is a necessary step toward a full and abundant life.

But it's not the only step.

If you want a future that is no longer doomed to become more of your past, then it is not enough to *believe* in Jesus' truth. You must also *align yourself* with that truth.

You must let go of the desire to rule your own life, because it hasn't worked in the past and you know it won't work in the future. Instead, you have to place yourself under God's authority, which, to be honest, is a much riskier step.

Even though it might sound illogical, giving up your personal desires, abandoning your current direction, aligning yourself with Jesus' life, and placing yourself under God's authority is the only way to experience true freedom.

SAME JOURNEY, NEW DIRECTION

The phone call came unexpectedly. The voice on the other end explained that he was a recruiter working for a church in Colorado. He was helping a church find a new lead pastor. I didn't think church headhunters even existed, but apparently I was wrong. At least one existed.

The headhunter asked if it was okay to send me a packet of information about the church, explaining its history, needs, and vision for the future. In a few days it arrived in the mail, and I sat at my kitchen table in Kentucky reading about a church that met in a tiny strip mall in Colorado. Its name was Flatirons Community Church. Still is.

At the time, I had no idea what a flatiron was, except that it was a cut of steak. Maybe there's a hibachi grill in the church? The packet explained that the Flatirons were a group of peaks on the Rocky Mountain Front Range just west of where the church met in Boulder County. The mountains look like those old pieces of iron that the pioneers heated up in order to press their flannel shirts and suspenders. Flatirons.

That packet came at an interesting time in my life. I had no direction. I had just walked through a season of frustration and confusion with my involvement in ministry. I made a deal with God to talk about real issues in real ways, but it was feeling increasingly impossible to pull that off. I felt like I was continually being shut down. Before I received the headhunter's phone call, I was talking with a friend about leaving the ministry and working for him. I would develop leaders for his chain of hotels. Great money. Lots of travel. Good perks.

Over the years, several churches had called me to see if I was interested in working with them, but none of them felt right. They all felt like the same house at a different address. Needless to say, I wasn't incredibly hopeful as I opened the packet about the church named after a pioneer's household appliance.

As I thumbed through the packet, I noticed a single phrase stamped on every page: "We exist to bring the awesome life of Christ to a lost and broken world."

That caught my eye. There are lots of churches floating around out there, and they exist for varying reasons, but most churches can't sit down and explain to you in a single, clear, and distinct sentence why they exist: "Um . . . we sing really old songs, learn about God stuff, and try not to go to hell. Oh! And also we try not to tick off the people who give us money. That one's important."

The people at Flatirons knew who they were and why they existed. Stamped on every piece of material in their informational packet was their bold declaration of why the church was created and the direction they were heading regardless of who they chose as their new lead pastor.

The Flatirons community was convinced that they existed to point people toward Jesus and his offer of the better life they were missing—not just survival but an awesome life. They were certain that this awesome life could only come through Jesus Christ and was available to the people who needed it the most: the lost and broken.

"We exist to bring the awesome life of Christ to a lost and broken world."

By now I was married to Robin, and that statement resonated with us for a couple of reasons. First, that was how we had already approached our twenty years of working with high school and college students. But more importantly, that was how we saw Jesus approaching his ministry. As we've already discussed, Jesus didn't bump into people to pass out judgment, explain which messes were acceptable and which weren't, or declare whom he loved and whom he hated. He simply made an awesome life available to lost and broken people.

I was one of the lost and broken people, so if there was a church that existed for the same reason that Jesus himself put on flesh and lived among us, then I wanted to be a part of it. After many interviews, dinners, and test runs, my family became a part of Flatirons Community Church, where I currently serve as lead pastor.

When that information about Flatirons came in the mail, I felt lost. I hadn't given up on God, but I was beginning to feel like he had given up on me. In the past, I had been convinced that I was supposed to be serving him in a church, but I had somehow lost that conviction. Just as I was about to walk away and work for a chain of hotels, God put a packet on my kitchen table and said, *Don't worry. You're still on my path. You thought I'd left, but I haven't gone anywhere. I've been preparing you for the next leg of our journey together. I've still got your future in my hands. Now grab your hiking boots and move to Colorado.*

In a season of life when I felt lost and abandoned, God grabbed my attention with a job offer from Colorado. He used it to remind me that, even though I might not know exactly where I'm headed, if I align my life with his plan, I can trust in his promise that the destination will be well worth it.

YOUR TRAIN TRACKS

The mountains of Colorado are very different from the corn and soybean fields of Indiana where I grew up. In my hometown, endless miles of railroad tracks crisscrossed the fields in order to haul off all that corn and soybean and turn it into, well, everything.

My little hometown didn't have much in the way of recreation or entertainment, so in the summer, my friends and I would hang out by the tracks. We did all the typical stuff, like having balancing competitions on the rails, flattening pennies under the giant engines, or throwing rocks at the passing train cars knowing that they couldn't stop to call our parents.

Sometimes when we were walking on the tracks, we'd begin to feel a rumble. Then a massive horn would sound out of nowhere warning all the stupid kids to get off the tracks. We'd all run like crazy for safety, but once we were off the tracks, we'd stop and stare down the train as it passed: *I ain't scared of you.* When all the cars rushed by, it was nearly hypnotic. The noise of the roaring wheels was deafening. The wind would swirl, our hearts would race, and we would try our hardest to look brave in front of that iron giant.

Every time a train roared by, I imagined where it had come from, where it was going, and what it was carrying.

Then, as quickly as the train had appeared, it vanished. Silence.

Even as an adult, I still think railroad tracks are cool. Think about it. Two pieces of track, each thousands of miles long, connect to thousands of other pieces of track and roll through thousands of small towns and cities. What fascinates me the most is, while they're incredibly long, the tracks never vary in width. They never waver, never separate, and never go their own way. If they ever do, disaster ensues.

I don't often visit my hometown anymore, but a few years ago, I had the opportunity to return to the place where my life began to take direction, for better or worse. While I was there, I took a walk on those old railroad tracks.

As I was balancing on the rails, I thought about my journey from being a weird kid from small-town Indiana to becoming the leader of a church in Colorado. I thought of all the joys and struggles that existed in between, and I realized that God had been with me the whole way. As I walked on those rails in my hometown, pretending to be a tightrope walker high above the Niagara Falls, I began to ponder life's tracks.

Everybody is on a track. Our individual tracks all come from different places, and they're all headed toward different horizons. They include everything that has ever happened to us—good and bad, pretty and ugly, our fault and someone else's. Our tracks have brought us precisely to the circumstances we are in today, and if we ride the same tracks into the future, it is inevitable that we can expect more of the same.

Your marriage is a result of the train tracks you've been riding. So are your friendships, jobs, attitudes, and family. Your life looks the way it does because of the minutes, hours, days, and years of track leading up to this moment. Will you be satisfied with more of the same?

Look around you. Examine yourself. Examine your finances, sexuality, addictions, good habits, and bad habits. Are you happy on this track? If nothing changes, if things keep heading the way they're headed, how do your relationships with your spouse, kids, friends, and parents end up? Is your future destined to mirror your past?

Perhaps for you, more of the past might be a good thing. But most of us know there is a difficult moment approaching when we are going to sound the horn, slam on the brakes, and realize we aren't at the destination we set out for. We aren't even close. We'll be confused because we were lied to. We had always been told that if we lived a certain way and stayed on a certain track, then our lives would be filled with happiness, contentment, meaning, and purpose. But they're not. We'll start to panic because we don't like where we're headed, but we also have no idea how to switch the tracks.

So what do we do when we want to change direction?

Most of us try to rev the engine. We do more, work harder, and move faster, thinking that if we can just push through the crappy stuff, then maybe something better is hiding just around the bend. We become the little engines who could: "I think I can, I think I can, I think I can . . ."

Many of us have had the following conversation with ourselves: "Next time, things will be different. If I work harder at this, everything will change. My next school year, relationship, job, marriage, or attempt at getting sober and starting over . . . they'll be different because I'm going to work harder at changing them." Don't act surprised when, five years down the road, you're still heading in the same direction. If you're on the same tracks, you'll get the same results.

Think about a time you've been lost. All "lost" scenarios have two factors in common. First, you never know exactly *when* you became lost. Second, when you finally realize you have no idea where you are or how to get back to familiar territory, running faster isn't going to help you. You need outside help. You need new guidance and a new direction.

A few years into our marriage, I was training for a series of triathlons. I had trained all spring and early summer for a race that was being held in Indiana. Immediately after the race, Robin and I planned to drive to Tennessee in order to spend the Fourth of July holiday on my sister's houseboat.

The race went well, which simply means I didn't die, so we loaded up the car and headed south for Tennessee.

There are two things you must know about my wife, Robin. First, whenever we get into the car, she immediately falls asleep. I'm not exaggerating. Five minutes into our trip, she was conked out, mouth open, sound asleep. Second, she can tend to be a distrusting person. So before she fell asleep, Robin asked, "Do you know where to turn off when we get to Nashville, or do you need me to stay awake and help you?"

She might as well have asked, "Are you a real man, or do you need me to show you how to drive?"

"Thanks, but I've got this," I replied. "Go to sleep."

In my opinion, Nashville is an incredibly confusing city. I've driven through Nashville hundreds of times, and every trip, the city is flooded with construction, detours, and poor signage. So I wound through the maze that is Nashville, Tennessee, and continued on my journey.

Eventually Robin woke up and asked where we were. "About an hour outside of Nashville," I replied.

At that exact moment, a massive green sign appeared on the horizon: Welcome to Alabama!

Obviously, I had missed a small (probably poorly marked) turn back in Nashville. Robin then began to shout words that I cannot repeat lest this book be banned from most Christian bookstores. In short, she made it clear that this was my fault.

I pulled over at a truck stop at the nearest exit. As I walked through the doors, it was like one of those scenes in a movie when someone who doesn't belong walks into an establishment and you hear the record player scratch as everybody stops to stare at you. The truck stop was filled with burly, good ol' Alabama boys, and I had forgotten that I hadn't changed from my triathlon. I was wearing hot pink running shorts, purple shoes, a running tank top, and I had shaved legs.

This would be no big deal in modern-day Boulder, Colorado, where running is the primary religion. But in Alabama, circa 1990, I quickly found myself in danger of getting the crap beat out of me.

I hurriedly asked for directions, ran back to the car, and drove away from Alabama as fast as possible.

Now, at the moment I realized I was lost, would it have helped if I were to press on the gas and continue in the same direction in hopes that I would wind up back in Tennessee? Of course not. No amount of good intentions, hard work, or determination would have put me back in Tennessee. I had to stop, find a new map, and head in a different direction.

I needed to switch my train tracks.

If you're unhappy with the train you're on, hear this truth: Jesus can change your direction. He can switch your tracks.

Please don't pretend that I just said Jesus is a quick, easy fix. The reality is that once you've put all your energy into pumping steam through that engine, and you have all that momentum hurtling the cars down the track, it takes a lot of time to slow down your train and change direction.

I'm also not talking about forgiveness from God. That was taken care of in the single event of Jesus dying on a cross. Your forgiveness, salvation, and standing with God have all been taken care of. I'm talking about your momentum. There's no such thing as, "All at once, everything was completely different." Yet Jesus died on a cross and rose from the dead so that he could help you make different decisions. You can't change your past no matter how sorry you are, but Jesus says your past doesn't have to condemn your future. He wants, over time, to change your momentum and point you toward a better life. He wants to free you from your dragons, even if it is going to take years to tear away the scales.

PUTTING YOURSELF UNDER
GOD'S AUTHORITY

How do you live a better life? Oddly enough, it looks a lot like a set of train tracks. Let me explain.

In the United States, train tracks are precisely four feet and eight-and-one-half inches apart. If one of the rails veers to the right or left, then so does the other, with constant precision and uniformity. Together they go up, and together they go down. The two rails never operate independently of each other. They are perfect companions.

Individually a rail can't do much, but as long as one sticks with the other and always runs parallel to it, train tracks can carry enormous, crushing amounts of weight over unbelievable distances.

Jesus operated the same way. He was one track and his Father was the other.

One time, some people asked Jesus, "Why do you do the things you do? Why do you run your life and make the decisions you do?" (paraphrased from the healing at the pool in John 5).

Jesus answered, "Very truly I tell you, the Son can do nothing by himself; he can do only what he sees his Father doing, because whatever the Father does the Son also does" (John 5:19).

Essentially Jesus said, "Why do I do the things I do? Well, the truth is that I can't do anything by myself. I can't do anything independently. I watch my Father. If my Father veers to the right, then so do I. If he veers to the left, then so do I. Together we go up, and together we go down. Wherever he's going, I want to go, too, and I know that if I ever separate from him, even fractionally, there's going to be a train wreck."

Jesus ran his life that way, and so should we. If God says

it, we should say it. If God does it, we should do it. If God wants something specific to happen in our lives or in our world, then we should want the same thing. We won't always understand why we're veering his direction, but we should veer regardless because we trust that God says it's a better way. This is called putting ourselves under God's authority.

When you put yourself under God's authority, you are stating that you're convinced God is good, loves you, wants the best for you, and will keep every promise he's ever made to you. You are stating that you're convinced following God means discovering an abundant life. You are promising to stick with God because to veer from him, even fractionally, will cause a train wreck.

If we're honest with ourselves, we can probably look back and realize we derailed our lives because we convinced ourselves we could reach a good destination using our own track. We went our own way, but not far down the road the sparks flew, the wheels broke contact, and our lives fell apart. That would describe almost every one of my personal mistakes and regrets.

Jesus knows we have this tendency, which is why he taught over and over that if you want a better, more awesome, and more abundant experience, then you need to line up your life parallel to God's instructions and commands. Jesus spent his whole life giving us the perfect example of what it looks like to run parallel to God.

Watch Jesus. Listen to him. Follow him. When he moves right, move right. When he moves up, move up. When he slows down, slow down. Whenever he runs, you run.

For some of us, this sounds confining: *This lifestyle sounds like an invasion of my privacy or the sacrifice of my free will. Doesn't it make me a slave to turn over control and authority to someone else?*

Well, yes and no.

When you align your track with Jesus', you remove yourself from the illusion that you can do life on your own, that your actions exist in a vacuum of no consequences. In this sense, yes, you forfeit authority over your own life by acknowledging this reality. But the result of placing yourself under the authority of God is quite the opposite of slavery and confinement.

One of the most frequently misquoted verses in the Bible is a quote from Jesus:

> Then you will know the truth, and the truth will set you free. (John 8:32)

That's a pretty famous verse, right? Many people quote this without even knowing it's from the Bible, let alone from Jesus himself. The issue here is that this is only half of Jesus' statement, and without the other half, the "truth" becomes open-ended. What truth will set you free? Where do you find this truth? The answer, of course, is "on the tracks," but you need to back up a verse in order to catch it.

Before Jesus said this, he had just dropped a heavy teaching on a group of people, and they were not happy. They began arguing with Jesus: "Who do you think you are to tell us what is right and what is wrong? What gives you the authority to tell us how to live our lives?" This carried on for quite a while. Some people ended up believing Jesus, and some did not. After the dust settled a bit, Jesus finally said:

> *If you hold to my teaching*, you are really my disciples. *Then you will know the truth*, and the truth will set you free. (John 8:31–32)

Did you catch that? Jesus made an if–then statement. *If* you hold to Jesus' truth and embrace it, only *then* will you know and experience the freedom of that truth. *If* he veers one direction and you veer the same, only *then* will you find yourself being led to freedom and the reality of a life that simply works better.

The Bible has something to say about veering the wrong direction. Solomon says:

> There is a way that appears to be right, but in the end it leads to death. (Proverbs 14:12)

You are free to veer the opposite direction of Christ. In some cases, it might even seem the right way to go, but in the end it won't work. Not because you're a bad person or you didn't try hard enough, but because, by definition, it's not the truth.

Jesus said there is a better way to live. You're not doomed to repeat train wreck after train wreck. Jesus said he could set you free from this cycle:

So if the Son sets you free, you will be free indeed. (John 8:36)

Nobody becomes a dragon overnight. We travel long roads comprised of twists, turns, mountains, and valleys in order to arrive where we stand. Then one day, we look in the mirror to find that we have gradually become monsters.

Jesus said, "I can reach into your dragon and set you free. I can pull you out of this mess, wash you, and lead you to the life you were created to live."

WHERE ARE YOU HEADED?

Pick out two or three of the most important areas in your life, like your family, friendships, marriage, career, romantic life, physical health, or emotional health. Now picture these important areas of your life rolling down the train tracks you've chosen. Five, ten, or twenty years down the road, where do they end up? Is that where you want them to be?

Let's get more specific. Imagine, in detail, the conversation that will take place when you come home from work and announce to your family, "I got fired because I did something really stupid and I got caught. Now you're all going to have to pay for my mistake. I'm sorry."

Imagine sitting down with the person you vowed to love more than anyone else in the world, the person you promised to remain faithful to until one of you died. Imagine telling that person, "I did something that is probably going to blow up our marriage and our family. I'm sorry, but nothing will ever be the same again."

Imagine walking into your child's bedroom like you've done a thousand times before, and they naively think you're going to tuck them in, tell them a story, and listen to their prayer. But instead, you're going to try to explain, "Mommy and Daddy will always love you, but we're not going to be one big family anymore."

Wake up. No matter how often you tell yourself, "My life is never going to end up there," the reality is that's where it has been, and if left unchecked, that's precisely where it's headed. No matter how much energy and speed you waste, your current track can only head one direction.

But there's another reality. Even if you never read another word from Jesus, I believe that you already know enough about his truth to take your first step toward aligning your life to his.

I'm not saying that you already know every change you need to make in your life. I'm not saying that your life is going to get better, fixed, or un-dragoned in three easy steps. I'm only saying, out of my own experience, that I bet you know at least one area of your life that Jesus wants you to align with his tracks. I'll even bet that you have a good idea of how to take those first few baby steps.

Unfortunately, I'm not saying that you will obey him and take those first steps. I'm only betting that you know what they are.

I suggest that you take a break from this book, take a walk, and have a long, difficult conversation with God *before* you decide to have a long, difficult conversation with anyone else on the planet. Ask him not only to show you what to do but to give you the strength to do it. You can ask him, in faith, to forgive your sins and mistakes. You can also ask him to give you the assurance that, even though you might not yet see how this could possibly lead to a better life, he will take care of you. You can ask him to help you trust.

Go. Take a walk on the train tracks of your life. Are you excited about where they might lead? Or can you see disaster around the next bend? Believing in Jesus' truth is useless without also switching to his tracks. Ask him for the desire, strength, and determination you need in order to run your life parallel to his.

4

ELEPHANTS, LIONS, AND DEPRESSION

What Happens When Dragons Hunt You?

In 1996, I had the incredible opportunity to visit Africa. I got to visit Kenya, *the* place to visit in Africa if you want to see the most famously dangerous animals in the world. The Primate Rescue Center of Nicholasville, Kentucky, has nothing on Kenya.

I was part of an advance trip with a few people who were scouting in Kenya to prepare for later mission teams. Our goal was to learn from, teach, and develop relationships with a tribe of people called the Massai. The trip became the first of many wonderful trips, and it served as the beginning of an awesome partnership with the Massai people.

The missionary who served as our tour guide on that trip was, well, kind of crazy. But in a good way. His name was Peter, and he was a cross between Jesus, the Crocodile Hunter, and Bear Grylls. In other words, he loved Jesus, but he would do the craziest, most incredible things when it came to the wilds of Africa.

Most of the time, if you want to see wild animals in Africa, you sign up for a commercial safari tour with a travel agent. You travel the same roads and routes that thousands of other tourists have explored. But if you were with Peter, you got an entirely different experience.

Peter wouldn't simply drive through the popular sightseeing routes and allow you to snap photos from a comfortable and safe distance. No. He would toss you in the truck and you would go off-roading into the middle of nowhere looking for anything with four legs. If you were lucky enough to stumble across a herd of some sort, there wouldn't be any quiet photography from the safety of the vehicle. Instead, you would hear Peter shouting, "Come on! Let's go!" as he leaped from the vehicle. You were then left with only two options. You could jump out and try to keep up with Peter, or you could stay in the truck as he disappeared into the tall grass and left you utterly alone in the African savanna with only your imagination to keep you company. Needless to say, you would end up sprinting toward Peter, praying, *Please help me, Jesus. This can't be happening.*

You think I'm exaggerating. I'm not.

On our first sightseeing adventure in Kenya, we tracked down herds of zebras and elephants. I learned about God's gift of camouflage to these creatures. When zebras sense danger, they dart in different directions, and the rapid flashing of their stripes leaves predators dazed like some kind of bad drug flashback. I also learned that the color of an elephant's hide matches that of the shade provided from the trees. One minute, an elephant the size of my house would be engulfing my field of vision. The next minute, it would move under the shade of a tree and completely disappear.

I learned a lot, and all of it was fascinating. But when you visit Africa, there is one particular animal you are hoping to see—the lion. When you get home, the first question out of everyone's mouths will not be, "Did you see an ostrich?"

So later in the trip, when Peter asked if I wanted to find any lions, I didn't have to think about it, pray about it, or weigh the pros and cons. My immediate answer was, "Yes! Let's go!" So we jumped in the truck, and this time we took a few local Massai guys with us to serve as guides. They stood in the back of the truck as we drove across the valley searching for giant cats.

Finding lions sounded easy. I mean, we were in Africa, right? I assumed that lions wandered right through everyone's front yards. It turned out it wasn't as easy as I had imagined. We drove for several hours without finding anything.

Just like elephants and zebras, God gave lions camouflage. God made lions the same color as the African grass. Not the green stuff that grows in our suburban front yards, but the tall, brown stuff that covers the savanna. The idea is that hungry gazelles will go out looking for something to eat, find a delicious clump of grass to dine on, walk over to grab a bite, but surprise! The delicious clump of grass will take a bite out of them.

We looked all day for signs of lions, but with no luck. We were about to call it quits when one of the Massai guys pounded on the roof of the truck, pointed to the horizon, and shouted something I didn't understand. Peter wheeled the truck in the same direction, and before long, we pulled up within a few feet of a pride of lions: one massive male lion and five females.

As I've already mentioned, I love animals. I had spent many hours watching television documentaries on various creatures, and I considered myself something of an expert. Lions, naturally, were one of my specialties. So I thought it wise to take the moment and do a bit of showing off. I began informing everybody in the truck about the responsibilities within the pride. I explained that the females were expected to do all the hunting and hard work, while the male was in charge of eating, breeding, and the occasional fight. I lectured everyone about the hunting habits, the mating habits, and the raising of the cubs. I thought I was quite impressive.

After exhausting all of the facts I knew about lions, I decided to do something that I now realize was dumb. At the time, my ADHD-ridden brain thought it would be a great idea to make direct eye contact with one of the four-hundred-pound lions and utter, "Meow!"

It didn't go well. In America, "meow" means little to nothing in cat language. But in Africa, "meow" apparently translates as, "Please, stand up and eat me." The moment "meow" came out of my mouth, that massive, grass-colored, wildebeest-eating, four-hundred-pound ball of muscle and teeth whipped her head around in my direction, dug her claws into the dirt, and tensed every inch of her body.

Nearly frozen in fear, I somehow managed to slowly roll up my window.

The Massai guys in the back of the truck started yelling, "Oobla, oobla, oobla," which I later learned translates as, "Stupid white guy!" They yelled for Peter to take off. As we were driving to safety, we looked behind us to see the entire pride of lions on their feet, peering at us as if to say, "Yeah, and if you know what's good for you, you won't come back."

Later that night, around the campfire, I received a heaping dose of well-deserved teasing about my so-called lion expertise, and during this conversation, Peter said something I have never been able to forget. When discussing our lion-hunting excursion, Peter said, "The tough part is not when you go hunting for lions. The tough part is when lions come hunting for you."

That statement has stuck with me because our dragons can be the same way.

Sometimes we make mistakes, and we end up becoming dragons. We do something stupid, make a series of bad choices, meow at something that can devour us, and before we know it, we are paying the price for our mistakes.

That reality is not easy to swallow, but at least it makes sense. That was my story. I had problems because I made mistakes. I hunted dragons.

But sometimes we don't necessarily do anything wrong or make any mistakes. As far as we can tell, we are doing exactly what we are supposed to be doing. We are genuinely pursuing Jesus, but our lives fall apart regardless. We are doing the right thing, and then, out of nowhere, a dragon appears from the tall grass and attacks us.

In these cases, we have no choice in the matter. We don't want it. We don't ask for it. We don't vote for it. The dragon stalks, ambushes, and swallows us up, and we left with the shredded remains of our lives. In this case, the dragons hunt us.

BEING THE HUNTED

What did Jesus call people who were attacked by dragons, regardless of the righteous way they were conducting their lives? Jesus called these people normal. Jesus made a few promises about what would happen to us, regardless of our faith. Here is what Jesus promised those who love him the most:

In this world you will have trouble. (John 16:33)

Jesus didn't say, "In this world, there is a slight chance that you will go through hard times." Jesus didn't say, "If you don't have enough faith, you will have trouble." Jesus didn't say, "If you go to church, stop cussing, don't drink too much, and always keep your promises, then you won't have any trouble."

Instead, Jesus said that trouble will hunt you. Period. If you are alive and breathing, you will have trouble in this world. Either you will hunt the dragon, or the dragon will hunt you. There is no escaping it.

Jesus had every right to make this statement. Jesus believed all the right things, and he had stronger faith and loved God more than you and I will ever be able to. Still, soon after making this statement, Jesus was arrested and nailed to a cross. Faith, belief, and love do not buffer or barricade your life from trouble and hardship. In fact, sometimes it feels like having faith and doing the right things can attract trouble.

I want to address the dragon that I most often see hunting the people around me: depression. This includes both the deep blues anyone can feel and the diagnosable imbalance that plagues so many. No one asks for this dragon, but he swallows up many people regardless. This dragon is big, heavy, overwhelming, and he has the potential to crush, suffocate, and swallow you up. This dragon doesn't create bad days or bad weeks. He creates bad childhoods, bad decades, and bad lives. On and on, day after day, year after year, this dragon causes pain with no relief in sight.

Remember that overwhelmingly sad feeling when you learned that someone you loved died? Remember the guilt and embarrassment you felt after your biggest failure was exposed? Remember facing the biggest problem in your life and thinking that it was impossible to fix? Remember that time, as a little kid, when someone held you under the swimming pool too long, and you thought you were going to drown?

Roll all of those emotions into one, carry them around with you every day from the time you wake up until the time you fall asleep, and you will begin to understand the dragon of depression.

When you experience the dragon of depression, your entire world is seen only through the lens of sadness, hopelessness, mourning, loss, emptiness, grief, pain, anger, frustration, guilt, and death. Death is always there, looming and lurking: "I can't live another minute like this. Death has to be better than this. The people around me would be better off if I wasn't here to hurt them. I can't do this anymore. This is never going to get any better."

The dragon of depression is a cyclical prison cell. It's like a dog chasing its own tail: "I am depressed. Because I'm depressed, I can't do what I need to do. This makes me feel like a failure. That makes me depressed. Because I'm depressed, I can't do what I need to do. This makes me feel like a failure. That makes me depressed."

David, the famous king from the Bible, knew these feelings well:

> *Have mercy on me, LORD, for I am faint;*
> *heal me, LORD, for my bones are in agony.*
> *My soul is in deep anguish.*
> *How long, LORD, how long?*
> *Turn, LORD, and deliver me;*
> *save me because of your unfailing love.*
> *Among the dead no one proclaims your name.*
> *Who praises you from the grave?*
> *I am worn out from my groaning.*

All night long I flood my bed with weeping
and drench my couch with tears. (Psalm 6:2–6)

How long, LORD? Will you forget me forever?
How long will you hide your face from me?
How long must I wrestle with my thoughts
and day after day have sorrow in my heart?
How long will my enemy triumph over me?
Look on me and answer, LORD my God.
Give light to my eyes, or I will sleep in death.
(Psalm 13:1–3)

King David wasn't alone, and you aren't either. This might surprise some readers, but Jesus understands what depression feels like. In the Garden of Gethsemane, just before Jesus was arrested, he experienced the height of his depression:

Then he said to them, "My soul is overwhelmed with sorrow to the point of death. Stay here and keep watch with me."

Going a little farther, he fell with his face to the ground and prayed, "My Father, if it is possible, may this cup be taken from me. Yet not as I will, but as you will." (Matthew 26:38–39)

If you read Hebrews 4:15, it is clear that Jesus had been tempted in every way that we are, yet he walked through those temptations without sinning. But somewhere along the way, it seems some biblical scholar or translator decided "depression" was no longer included in the long list of ways that Jesus was tempted.

In my opinion, it's tough to read, "My soul is overwhelmed with sorrow to the point of death" without concluding that Jesus was struggling with depression. Jesus essentially said, "I've been swallowed up to the core of my being with sorrow. The suffocating weight of my sadness is about to crush my life." Elsewhere, the Bible says this about Jesus' time in the garden:

> Being in anguish, he prayed more earnestly, and his sweat was like drops of blood falling to the ground. (Luke 22:44)

There is a medical condition (hematidrosis) brought on by extreme emotional anguish, strain, and stress during which the capillaries in the skin rupture, allowing blood to flow out of a person's sweat pores. So for hours, alone in a dark corner of a remote garden, Jesus fell down, curled up on the ground, cried, and prayed so intensely for deliverance from his circumstances that the blood vessels burst inside his skin. You can call it whatever you want, but to me it looks like emotional depression.

Jesus understood, and still understands, depression.

Weeks before Jesus was in the garden, he came face-to-face with everything I've just described. I've already touched on this story in chapter 2, but let's take a quick look again:

> They went across the lake to the region of the Gerasenes. When Jesus got out of the boat, a man with an impure spirit came from the tombs to meet him. This man lived in the tombs, and no one could bind him any more, not even with a chain. For he had often been chained hand and foot, but he tore the chains apart and broke the irons on his feet. No one was strong enough to subdue him. Night and day among the tombs and in the hills he would cry out and cut himself with stones. (Mark 5:1–5)

Depression can be caused by many different things. In this guy's case, depression was caused by satanic attack or demonic oppression. The man in this story was possessed by many demons. If you're anything like me, you immediately think of *The Exorcist* or some sci-fi movie, but the reality is that, all through the Bible, we read descriptions of battles being fought in the spiritual realm. The New

Testament teaches that while a Christian cannot be possessed by Satan or one of his demons, he *can* be oppressed. Satan continues to wage war against Christians by attacking or tempting us.

Depression can also be caused by guilt. Sometimes the weight of our downfalls and sins can cause us to grieve and mourn to the point of depression. That's one of the reasons King David was depressed. He had just been convicted of adultery and murder, and his child was about to die. He used phrases like, "My bones wasted away . . . my strength was sapped. . . . Do not forsake me, my God. . . . My heart has turned to wax . . . my tongue sticks to the roof of my mouth. . . . Troubles without number surround me" (Psalm 32:3–4; 71:18; 22:14–15; 40:12).

The apostle Peter understood depression after he denied knowing Jesus. After his sin of denying Jesus, Peter wept bitterly (Matthew 26:75). Judas understood depression after he betrayed Jesus to his death. When the weight and guilt of what he had done finally hit him, Judas decided that committing suicide was the only way out of the belly of the dragon in which he found himself swallowed (Matthew 27:1–5).

Depression can also be caused by the difficult circumstances of our lives. Life can get so hard that it makes us depressed, and that's what Jesus was feeling in the Garden of Gethsemane. He understood why he needed to be sacrificed.

He even knew the wonderful outcome that would result from his torture and death. Yet even though Jesus knew that the next few days would ultimately become the most wonderful event ever to occur in the history of the universe, the thought of them still caused him to collapse to the ground, curl up, and cry until blood seeped from his pores.

Depression can also be the result of a physical illness. Sometimes the circumstances of our bodies can cause us to become depressed. I'm not talking about body image issues causing someone to become depressed (although that happens often). I'm talking about synapses misfiring and chemicals becoming imbalanced. I'm talking about diseases within our bodies. This can be the most difficult cause of depression to wrestle with because you can't quite put your finger on the reason you are suffering. You're simply suffering. More on this in a minute.

Regardless of the cause of depression, one factor remains constant: depression always centers on death and pain.

Depression is about death. The naked guy on the beach in Mark 5 lived in a cemetery. When you feel dead inside, you begin to dwell on the things of death, and eventually that place becomes your home. Depression is also about pain. The man would cry out and cut himself with razor-sharp stones.

I know a woman named Lisa. When she was a child,

her mother committed suicide while Lisa was in the same room. Lisa blamed herself for her mother's death: *If I had only been a better daughter . . . I should have done something to save my mom.* None of these thoughts were valid, but in her five-year-old mind, they were the conclusions Lisa drew.

Lisa was then adopted, but her adoptive father sexually molested her from the time she was eight years old until she was in middle school. Lisa's adoptive mother refused to step up, protect Lisa, acknowledge her pain, or give her comfort. Lisa's adoptive mother eventually told Lisa to get over it and not tell anyone. Her adoptive father was never confronted or brought to justice. To this day, the family tries to pretend that it never happened.

As a result, over the next ten years, Lisa looked for love, healing, and comfort in all the wrong places. She gave birth to three or four babies from different fathers, and she had four abortions that I know of, maybe more. She attempted suicide several times, she self-medicated with drugs and alcohol, and she had scars all up and down her arms and legs from where she had cut herself with knives, razors, pins, and glass. She identified with the words of the song "Hurt" by Nine Inch Nails, in which the singer describes the pain of self-inflicted harm as "the only thing that's real."[1]

Depression has many causes, it revolves around death and pain, and it has no easy fixes. For both the man living in the cemetery and Lisa, no one could fix them. No one was smart or strong enough. As soon as they believed they had the demon, the sickness, and the depression captured and controlled, it would break through and overwhelm once again.

Let's continue with the story about the naked man on the beach:

> When he saw Jesus from a distance, he ran and fell on his knees in front of him. He shouted at the top of his voice, "What do you want with me, Jesus, Son of the Most High God? In God's name don't torture me!" For Jesus had said to him, "Come out of this man, you impure spirit!"
>
> Then Jesus asked him, "What is your name?"
>
> "My name is Legion," he replied, "for we are many." (Mark 5:6–9)

Later in this story, Jesus sends the spirits away and heals the man. That's when the crowd shows up:

> When they came to Jesus, they saw the man who had been possessed by the legion of demons, sitting there, dressed and in his right mind; and they were afraid. (Mark 5:15)

Jesus is bigger, stronger, and Most High over everything. In the story about the naked man at the beach, the demon of depression recognized and yielded to the authority of Jesus. Jesus is bigger than depression.

Whether you personally hunted down your dragon or it stalked and ambushed you, Jesus can set you free again.

ROBIN'S DRAGON

Here is where this chapter could detour into a bunch of tired religious slogans and promises like, "If you just have faith and pray, then God will take your problems away." Don't worry. That's not where we are headed.

I want to share one more story with you. This is a story that hits very close to home for me. In fact, it is the reason I just spent an entire chapter talking about the taboo subject of depression and Christianity. This isn't the story of some guy in the Bible. This isn't the story of some person I knew in Kentucky.

This is the story of Robin, the sea otter at swim practice. Robin is the one who dragged me to church. Robin is the reason I bumped back into Jesus. Robin is the person I love more than anyone else on the planet. Robin is my wife. Robin is my best friend.

Robin is also bipolar. The dragon of depression has stalked Robin all of her life.

I will let her tell her own story:

Hi, my name is Robin Burgen, and I'm bipolar, or manic-depressive. I've started with the words of a twelve-step program because Jesus described the church as a hospital for sick or broken people—a place where people can be real, authentic, imperfect, and flawed as well as accepted, supported, loved, and cared for. Everybody needs a place like this.

Wonderful Christian parents raised me. I wasn't abused. I didn't have a bad childhood, and there's no deep, dark, painful secret in my past to explain why I'm bipolar. I grew up in the church. I had a Five-Year Perfect Attendance pin in Sunday school when I was only six years old.

Looking back, the first time I remember depression striking was during my junior year of college. Coincidentally, that's about the same time I started dating Jim . . . hm. I went to the counselor and told him that I was going home because I didn't have the strength to get out of bed. He talked to me and helped me deal with some grief issues surrounding the death of my dad. Things got better for a while. After the birth of each of my children, I suffered severe bouts of depression, but I wrote them off as postpartum blues.

Life really came crashing down shortly after we moved to Louisville, Kentucky, when Jim got a job as a senior high pastor. I remember showing up to church on my thirtieth birthday—a crowded church, a crowded parking lot, and two preschool children in the rain—and thinking, *Why are all these people smiling?*

I tried to fake it for a while, but after returning from a mission trip in Jamaica, things began to fall apart fast. I retreated to my bedroom—my cocoon— and I pulled the blankets over my head. I began to shut down. Before long, my only goal was to be out of bed and dressed before my kids came home from school. When I couldn't, Jim did his best to explain to the kids that Mommy was "sad in her heart," and they did their best to understand.

Depression is lonely. I just couldn't be around people. They were happy, and I wasn't. I didn't have the energy anymore to pretend. After stiff-arming people, turning down invitations, or simply not showing up because of the depression, everybody quit calling and inviting. We were always saying no. After a while, we didn't have any friends, although friends were what we needed. But we couldn't understand what was happening, so how could we expect anyone else to understand?

Work was impossible. How many times can you call your boss and say, "Hey, I can't make it in today. I'm too sad"? I stopped going to church, I began missing my kids' programs and games, and I shut down further and further. As I sank deeper into the pit, Jim went into function mode. He had to be both mother and father for the kids. He cooked, he cleaned, he carpooled, and he tried to run a youth ministry. Jim is a fixer. When he saw that I was depressed, his first response was to clean the house or do the laundry, thinking, *Maybe that will make her feel better.* It didn't. It only made me feel even guiltier.

I wasn't the person I wanted to be, the wife I wanted to be, the mom I wanted to be, or the Christian I wanted to be. I began to think, *I'm ruining everyone's life. They would be so much better off without me.* I wanted to die. I thought about it all the time.

Things came to a head on a Wednesday afternoon. Jim came home from lunch to find me wedged between my bed and the wall in hysterics. I was begging God to let me die. I couldn't do it anymore. My doctor put me in the hospital to try adjusting my medications. This gave me a temporary break from performing, but I knew I'd have to go home soon. The next several years were a roller coaster of emotions, psychiatrists, doctors, and constantly changing medications. Nothing ever worked well for long.

My form of depression has two phases. One is a manic, or hyperactive, phase where I get a little crazy. I can't sleep, my mind races, and I become obsessive and compulsive. Looking back, my family and I can laugh at some of it. Like the time I was feeling really manic, and I wrapped all our Christmas presents in an hour at four in the morning. Or the time I found a book called *Cooking for a Month* and cooked all the food in the house in a single afternoon.

Most of the time, however, I was in the depression phase. I would stay in bed, cry, and feel like I wanted to die. Sometimes the medication took away my ability to feel anything at all. Someone once asked me if there were any warning signs that depression was going to hit. That is one of the worst things—I never know what tomorrow will be like. Depression is always there, waiting to ambush me. I can't plan. I can't count on anything. Good days make it worse because I know it's only a matter of time. Sometimes I hate to go to sleep because I don't know what I'm going to wake up to tomorrow.

Then came the day. I was home alone, exhausted, worn out from trying, and angry. I was very angry with God. I had done everything I was supposed to do. I had gone to Christian counselors and a Christian psychiatrist. I had done everything they told me to do. I had prayed, and I had been faithful. So where was God? I thought he owed me. Why wasn't he taking care of me? I knew what the promises were, so why wasn't God holding up his end of the bargain?

I began to pray aloud, sobbing. I was done. I cried out to God. I even screamed at him, "God, do your job!" But I didn't even have the words to tell him my pain. I was only groaning. I told God, "Someone has got to pray for me. I can't even do it anymore. I can't say what I need to say. I don't know what to pray for anymore."

It was at that moment that I felt Jesus wrap his arms around me. I knew, at that moment, Jesus was interceding for me before the Father. I knew Jesus was praying for me, just like it says in the book of Romans. I could feel it. I felt comfort—a comfort that I can't describe. And peace. I felt peace for the first time in a long, long time.

I wish I could wrap up my story with a nice, pretty bow. I wish I could say, "I got up off that couch, and I never fought depression again," but that's not what happened.

I fight depression every day, even now. But I'm reminded of what Paul says in 2 Corinthians 12:8–10: "Three times I pleaded with the Lord to take it away from me. But he said to me, 'My grace is sufficient for you, for my power is made perfect in weakness.' Therefore I will boast all the more gladly about my weaknesses, so that Christ's power may rest on me. That is why, for Christ's sake, I delight in weaknesses, in insults, in hardships, in persecutions, in difficulties. For when I am weak, then I am strong."

So . . . my story goes like this. My name is Robin Burgen, and I battle depression every day. I have asked God to heal me. His response, so far, has been no. "No, but my grace is sufficient for you, and I will go through this with you."

Some days are good, and some days are horrible. Sometimes the medicine works. Sometimes it doesn't. But when I am weak, he is my strength, and when I run out of words to pray, he even prays for me.

In the Bible, there is a long list of people who lived their entire lives looking forward to the promises of God but died before they saw them fulfilled. God commended them for their faith. I know now that God doesn't owe me anything, but he will keep his promises. I know that someday God will heal me. If not in this life, then definitely when I meet him face-to-face. Until that time, I will live trusting his promises that he is always with me, he will never forsake me, and he is my strength when mine is gone.

Robin is my hero.

Robin did everything she was supposed to. She had faith, and she loved God. Her mess wasn't the result of bad choices and decisions. She didn't go looking for trouble.

Instead, trouble found her. Dragons hunted Robin. In her case, the dragon of depression and emotional anguish hunted her down and swallowed her whole. The dragon robbed her of years of her life.

Here is what God has been teaching Robin and me through this. No matter how you get swallowed by a dragon, when you reach the point where all seems lost and you finally scream out, "God, where are you?" you will find an answer. Eventually you will realize God was there all the time.

Before I met Robin, I made a lot of stupid decisions, and I went looking for trouble. I hunted dragons. Eventually I found them, and they swallowed me whole. Years later, when I no longer wanted anything to do with the dragon I had become, Jesus reached into my mess, pulled me out, and set me free.

The truth is that your story could go either way. I hate to say that, but it's true. You could make a ton of bad choices and wind up hunting the dragon that will consume your life. You could also do everything right and try your best to protect yourself from dragons, but in the end, have them devour you anyway.

But I won't leave you hanging with, "Sorry, pal. That's just the way it is." Instead, we're going to wade into a couple of large and looming questions:

- If God sometimes allows dragons to hunt and pursue us, then is he still a good God?
- And if in this world there will be trouble, then what is the point of having faith?

5

SHARK WEEK, ALLERGIES, AND FAITH

Faith Isn't What You Thought It Was

Becoming a pastor was not on my to-do list. In fact, through-out life, I've held on to a different dream and vision. I've held so tightly to this dream that, if the elders of Flatirons were to enter my office tomorrow and say, "Thanks, Jim. It's been a good run, but we think it's time for you to hang it up," I'd be disappointed, but I wouldn't be completely dev-astated. Because I know precisely what I would do with my life. I would become a park ranger.

I would sell everything I own, jump in my Jeep, head to the mountains, build a small cabin, and hire myself out to anyone who needed directions to the nearest picnic area, elk herd, or hiking trail. I would sport one of those cool park ranger hats like the guy from the Yogi Bear cartoon. I would tell people interesting facts like how all the trout wound up in the mountain streams, why Canadian geese have unique migrating habits, and how to survive an encounter with a mountain lion on the trail (the answer, by the way, is to run faster than at least one person).

My closet desire to become a park ranger dates back to when I was a kid and we only had three television stations to choose from (four, if the weather was nice and we wrapped a big wad of tinfoil around the rabbit-eared antennae on top of our gargantuan TV set). One of those few channels broadcast my all-time favorite show: *Mutual of Omaha's Wild Kingdom*. The show featured an old guy named Marlin Perkins, who shared fun facts about wild animals, occasionally interrupted by sales pitches for home, auto, and life insurance.

The best part of the show featured Marlin's assistant, whose name was . . . Jim! I could hardly believe the stroke of good luck that allowed me to share his name. Jim would do incredible things like dive out of helicopters, tackle enormous snakes or crocodiles, and check zebras for unmentionable kinds of diseases in unmentionable kinds of places. As Jim fearlessly wrestled these dangerous creatures, Marlin's voice would narrate the encounter: "Watch out, Jim! Those teeth look sharp!" As a kid, I wanted to be Jim. Not little Jimmy from Indiana, but big Jim from *Mutual of Omaha's Wild Kingdom.*

Alas, it wasn't meant to be. But you can imagine how excited I was as an adult when we were finally able to afford cable, and I discovered some of God's greatest gifts to mankind: Animal Planet, the Discovery Channel, and the National Geographic Channel, just to name a few. And just in case those channels didn't stream enough awesomeness from the glow of our television sets, some genius took it to a whole new level by blessing our living rooms with a fierce and marvelous phenomenon: Shark Week.

There are few moments better than experiencing your first Shark Week: an entire week of programming on the Discovery Channel that features facts about different species of sharks, and better yet, stories about people's horrifying encounters with these deadly creatures.

Shark Week is incredible in and of itself, but I love that week for another reason as well. Maybe it's because I've been a pastor for too long and I now see everything through a metaphorical lens, but during last year's Shark Week, God taught me something about dragons, myself, Jesus, and faith.

SHARK-ATTACK FAITH

I was watching a show called *Dangerous Encounters* or something like that. The show is a compilation of stories from people who have been attacked by sharks but lived to tell about it, scars and all. On one particular episode, a father and son had been playing in the surf of the Atlantic Ocean on the coast of Florida. Come to find out, this stretch of coastline is the shark-attack capital of the world. Ironically, it's the same beach where Robin and I spent our honeymoon (note to self: don't ever use that travel agent again). Anyway, no one bothered to share that important fact with this family, and it quickly ruined their summer vacation.

Toward the end of one of their seemingly perfect vacation days, the father and son decided to catch a few more waves before calling it quits. However, on this last outing, a shark latched onto the boy's leg. As the boy screamed, the father grabbed his arm, and for the next several seconds, a life-or-death tug-of-war broke out between the father and the bull shark. Eventually the shark let go, the father carried his bleeding son to the beach, someone called 911, and the boy was flown by helicopter to a nearby hospital where he was rushed to surgery.

In the hospital waiting room, a large crowd of family and church members had gathered to hold hands and pray for the boy. In the background, you could overhear bits and pieces of those prayers. You could hear phrases like, "Father, we believe you are going to heal our little boy," or "We claim your promise that nothing will harm those who have true faith," or "Jesus, I know you are going to deliver our boy from the valley of the shadow of death."

Eventually the doctor entered through the big, swinging doors and announced that, although the boy had lost a ton of blood and would have a long recovery and rehabilitation, he was going to be just fine.

The parents, family, and church members then began crying, hugging, and shouting things like, "Thank you, Jesus! Praise God!" Shortly after this celebration, the interviewer asked the mother for her thoughts and feelings. The mom responded, "We just never gave up the faith. We believed that God was going to make everything work out. We knew that God was going to take care of our boy. If you have enough faith, then life will always work out like God promised."

The end.

First of all, let me say that I think it's great the little boy lived through the shark attack and the following surgery. I will also say that, if a shark bit my son, I would probably behave just like the family in the hospital waiting room. I would want every individual at my church to hit his or her knees and pray for my son's recovery. In short, I don't want to take anything away from that hurting family's experience in Florida.

However, I have to admit, when I saw that episode of *Dangerous Encounters*, I had only one thought running through my mind. Maybe it was because I was preparing to teach on the subject of faith at Flatirons in a few days, or maybe it was because my own faith was being stretched and challenged at that particular time. Regardless, as I watched that family's story unfold on my television screen, my first and only thought was simply, *What if the boy had died?*

I'm not trying to be a downer or a cynic, but what should we have concluded about faith if the boy had died in the jaws of the shark or on the operating table? The mother claimed that her boy recovered because of her and her husband's faith. Does that mean if the boy died, it was because his mom and dad did *not* have enough faith? Is that how faith works?

Let's take this logic a step further. I have been in many hospital emergency rooms. I've sat in waiting rooms, trying to comfort parents whose children are sick or in surgery due to everything from cancer to car wrecks. We've prayed those same kinds of prayers for our kids, but they never got better. Instead, they eventually got worse and died. Does this mean that we didn't have as much faith as the parents of the boy who was attacked by the shark? Is that how faith works?

Let's take it even further. The mother claimed that, in response to her faith and prayers, God kept his promise and spared her boy's life. Does this mean if the boy died, it would be because God either wouldn't or couldn't keep his promises? Is that how faith works?

Here's the kicker: if the boy's parents had so much faith, then why didn't God keep the shark away from their kid in the first place?

THE MAGIC FAITH FORMULA

I would love to tap into the type of faith that keeps bad stuff away in the first place, wouldn't you? The type of faith that repairs or heals my life when bad stuff happens is okay, I guess. But I want the kind of faith that keeps sharks, cancer, and car wrecks away. I want the kind of faith that ensures I will always have what I need, and better yet, what I want. I want the kind of faith that makes sure my bills get paid, the people I love stay healthy, and my kids make it home safely every night.

To be honest, I want to have the kind of faith I hear about when I secretly watch late-night religious television programs. You know, the shows where the preacher with a bad mullet, freakishly white teeth, and tears streaming down his cheeks promises you that if you send him—I mean, the ministry—a hundred dollars as a "faith offering," then God will repay you ten times over.

According to those religious television shows, that kind of faith works. We've all heard the testimonies: "My name is Bob. I was spending a Friday night at home alone, reading my Bible while all my coworkers were out at the bars doing God knows what with promiscuous women. I simply had faith and prayed that God would one day bring me the right woman. Just as I said, 'Amen,' I heard a loud car crash in my front yard. I ran outside to discover a wonderful, young, Christian supermodel in the car. It was love at first sight! We've been married for twenty glorious years! All you need is faith!"

Or how about this one: "My name is Susan. I was living on the street. I was hungry, homeless, and hopeless, but I still had my faith. I found a dollar on the street one day, and I prayed, *Dear Lord, what do you want me to do with this dollar?* The Lord told me to send it to this ministry, so I did. The next day I won the lottery, and I'm now a millionaire! All you need is faith!"

Awesome. So you're saying that if I'm broke, lonely, or sick, then all I have to do is tap into Jesus' "magic faith formula" in order to make all my wishes come true? If that faith exists, I'm in! Sign me up.

If we're honest with ourselves, this is the kind of faith we are hunting for. We're searching for the kind of faith that, when magically tapped into, will bring us the lives we've always wanted. We're looking for a formula or combination that will unlock the secret code that forces God to do things for us. We are searching for if-then faith: "If I do this right and do it enough, then God will be forced to bless me, even if he wasn't originally planning to. He will have to because I 'faithed' him."

There is no shortage of people standing in pulpits or streaming through cable TV into your living room claiming they've discovered the magic faith formula that will deliver all the results you've ever hoped for. This approach to faith is like a slot machine.

Go to church three times a week, pray twice a day, and put a dollar in the bucket. Pull. Nothing.

Go to church four times a week, pray three times a day, and put two dollars in the bucket. Pull. Nothing.

Go to church five times a week, pray four times a day, put five dollars in the bucket, give up smoking, do the hokey pokey and turn yourself around. Pull. This time, something happened! So you file that formula away and tell yourself that you've figured out what it takes to get God to do whatever you want. You keep practicing this formula, and for a while, life keeps going your way.

But one day, when you need something big to happen, you return to your formula, and this time nothing happens. Now what? You're confused. You thought you had discovered the secret formula. What's wrong? Why did God quit working for you? With this version of faith, there can only be one of two answers: there's either something wrong with God, or there's something wrong with you.

Let's look at option one: *There's something wrong with God.* If you had the faith formula figured out, then God should have made your prayers come true. So if God chose not to answer your prayers, then that makes God mean. And if God wanted to make it happen but he couldn't, then that makes God weak. I find it difficult to have faith in a God that is either weak or mean.

Let's look at option two: *There's something wrong with you.* Maybe you're doing something wrong. Maybe you're not doing enough, and if you simply prayed more often or gave up a few more bad habits, then maybe God would respond to your faith and work harder for you. Maybe you have some sin in your life that is keeping God from working for you. Maybe he's holding a grudge against you for stuff you did back in college. Maybe he is punishing you. Or even worse, maybe he is tired of you, he has given up on you, and he never really loved or cared about you in the first place. Maybe you are on your own because if you had the right kind of faith, then obviously God would have given you everything you've ever wanted.

There are too many people preaching this version of faith. In fact, this version of faith is why many of us have either lost our faith or are trying to decide if we have faith anymore. The majority of us have experienced the letdown that envelops this type of faith. We desperately needed God to pull through, so we asked God to fix something, but he didn't. In fact, it only got worse. We used the faith formula we thought we were supposed to use, and it didn't work. So now we're left to connect the dots on our own.

How can life be hard but God be good? Why do bad things happen to good people? If God is good, then why did he allow terrible things to happen in our lives? Why didn't he stop them? When life delivers something painful or confusing, our first response is often to look at God and shout, "Why is this happening?" Of course, we are actually asking, "Why did *you let* this happen?"

When you look back at the times you have thrown up your hands in frustration with God and have been tempted to say, "Screw it. I'm done with this whole God thing," aren't they usually the moments when you can't understand how to align what you believed God ought to have done with what he actually did?

Eventually we will all find ourselves sitting in a hospital waiting room, funeral home, police station, or lawyer's office, and we will have to ask ourselves whether or not God is still in all of this. We will have to ask ourselves why he allowed certain disasters to occur. We will have to ask ourselves if we can still believe in a God who lets bad things happen.

For many of us, in those moments, we let go of true faith and we go rogue: "If this is how God takes care of people, then I'm better off on my own. I needed God to help me, I begged him to intercede, and he did nothing. If God is not going to help me, then who needs him? I'll just do it by myself. If this is God, faith, church, religion, truth, a better way, or whatever you want to call it, then I quit. I'm out."

In those moments, we will be tempted to ask ourselves, "How can I believe in a God like this?" and we won't have the answer. Some of us will struggle because we feel we can't put a God who claims to be good alongside our current circumstances and have both of them make sense. Our faith will begin to collapse.

Personally, when I look over my life, especially at the moments when I moved in directions that led to most of the bad decisions that turned me into a dragon, I can see that I often pointed the finger at other people and blamed them for my circumstances: "That guy hurt me. That girl embarrassed me. That person was supposed to take care of me, but he or she didn't." The list goes on and on.

However, in my most monumental moments of frustration and desperation, the only person I'm pointing my finger at is God: "Thanks for nothing! Hey, God! Do your job better! Are you even paying attention? Why won't you help me out? I thought you were supposed to take care of me. Apparently I was wrong. If this is what life is like with you, and if this is what faith gets me, I'm just as well fending for myself."

In those moments, I jump the tracks and begin heading the way of the dragon. Sound familiar?

WHEN TOWERS CRUMBLE

One of my favorite moments from Jesus' life is contained in a short paragraph that I often read through quickly, wrinkle up my forehead with a what-is-that-supposed-to-mean look, and leave behind in search of something that makes more sense. The story is found in Luke 13.

Years earlier, upon entering the temple to offer sacrifices to God, some people were murdered and their blood was mixed with their sacrifices in order to ridicule their faith. In other words, they were doing something that God had commanded them, and it got them killed. Jesus knew exactly what people were thinking: *Why did this terrible thing happen to such good people?*

In response, Jesus posed the question that everyone else was too afraid to ask:

> Jesus answered, "Do you think that these Galileans were worse sinners than all the other Galileans because they suffered this way?" (Luke 13:2)

Jesus knew that everybody was wondering why the good guys so often suffer and die. They were wondering why God either allowed them to die or refused to protect their lives. So Jesus asked, "Do you think God zapped these guys because of some secret, horrible sin in their lives that only he knew about?"

Then he cut to the chase and answered his own question.

I tell you, no! (Luke 13:3)

Jesus made it clear: the reason those people died had nothing to do with their sinful behavior or lack of faith. Jesus then steered the conversation a whole new direction.

But unless you repent, you too will all perish. (Luke 13:3)

In other words, Jesus said, "You people are asking whether or not these guys were murdered because God was punishing them for something they did wrong. The answer is no. But let me turn this around and ask you something. If you were in the same horrible circumstances, and if you were murdered in the temple, would you have been ready to meet God?" Jesus continued:

Or those eighteen who died when the tower in Siloam fell on them—do you think they were more guilty than all the others living in Jerusalem? I tell you, no! But unless you repent, you too will all perish. (Luke 13:4–5)

A tower had collapsed and killed eighteen guys in the town of Siloam, and everybody was trying to figure out why it happened. They were asking themselves why God had allowed the tragedy to occur, and they were questioning whether or not God had viewed it as the perfect opportunity to take his giant finger and squash out eighteen sinners in one fell swoop.

Once again, Jesus answered his own question. No, those men did not die because of their sin or lack of faith. Again, Jesus turned the conversation back on the people. He asked if they would have been ready to meet God if the tower had fallen on them instead.

For me, there are two incredibly important pieces to this story that deserve our attention. First, Jesus taught that every time something bad or painful happens, we're not supposed to assume that God is punishing or zapping people because they are sinners. Christians are infamous for suggesting this. Whenever you turn on the news to learn about a tornado, hurricane, earthquake, wildfire, or tsunami that has ravaged a part of the world, it is only a matter of minutes before some Christian "expert" jumps in front of the camera and declares that the natural disaster is a result of God's judgment on sinners. I want to push them out of the camera's focus and yell, "Don't listen to this religious quack! He has no idea why this happened."

If Jesus, who was the only person on earth qualified to explain the secrets of life, never explained the tragedies we experience, then I'm sure it is safe to say that some Bible-thumping, finger-pointing, know-it-all nut job on television doesn't have the authority to explain any tragedies.

This leads me to the second important piece of this story that I think we need to pay attention to: Jesus didn't explain why the murders or the tower collapse happened. Jesus didn't end up saying, "Well, it's not because they were bad people, but let me explain what's really going on. The tower fell over and killed those men because . . ."

Nope. He didn't explain why. He simply said, "The reason for that tower falling over is not what you think it is, and it's not yours to worry about."

If Jesus needed to explain the causes of that tragedy to us, he would have. If he thought it would have helped us, he would have explained everything. But he didn't. Instead, he began a more important conversation: "I don't want you to think about why the tower fell on those men. I want you to think about where you would stand with God if the tower had fallen on you."

WHAT FAITH *ISN'T*

When something goes wrong in our own lives or the lives of the people we care about, our first typical response is to look up at God and demand that he explain himself to us. We want God to lay out his blueprint on the table so that we can decide whether or not we like how he's putting it all together.

However, if we're honest with ourselves, we'll admit that having an answer to the question, "Why have you done this?" wouldn't be helpful at all. In the most devastating moments of our lives, there will never be an answer or explanation that will take away all of the pain and make us feel content with the tragedies we're experiencing.

Here's an example on a smaller level. When my son, Jordan, was three years old, he was allergic to pretty much everything: dairy, corn, soy, wheat, you name it. Try shopping in the grocery store for a food that doesn't contain one of those elements in some form or extract. Needless to say, Jordan was always fighting a cold, ear infection, or stomachache. Finally, Robin loaded him in the car seat and drove him to the doctor's office.

Jordan had always enjoyed Dr. Tom's company. Dr. Tom would try to convince Jordan that he could hear Mickey Mouse inside his chest. Not to overspiritualize my son, but during one doctor visit, Jordan corrected Dr. Tom by stating, "Mickey Mouse is not in my heart. Jesus is in my heart." Don't get too excited. I'm sure Jordan followed this statement by eating a thermometer or grabbing a nurse inappropriately.

Anyway, Jordan's expectations for a fun-filled doctor's visit were soon extinguished as he was whisked into a room, stripped of his clothes, and pinned down by his mother and two nurses while, for the next thirty minutes, the doctor systematically stuck needles into the tender skin on Jordan's back in order to see which substances would cause a negative reaction in his body.

That evening, Robin tearfully related the story to me. As Jordan lay there, screaming and sobbing from the pain, he managed to turn his head toward Robin and cry out, "Mommy, no! Make it stop!" Then, in desperation, believing this doctor visit to be punishment for something he had done wrong, Jordan whimpered, "I'm sorry. I'll be good."

Most of you reading this understand that, while this was tough for Jordan and Robin to endure, it was also the right thing to do. You would say that Robin was being a good mom. Most of you would even go so far as to say that had Robin chosen not to take Jordan to the doctor and put him through that series of painful tests, she would have been a negligent mom. I would agree with you. Part of being a good parent is doing everything possible to ensure that your child will experience a healthy childhood.

But from Jordan's perspective, none of that made sense. What you and I would claim to be logical, healthy, and sound parenting, Jordan would have called senseless torture. To Jordan, that doctor visit was punishment, not provision. As Jordan looked into the face of his mom, he genuinely believed that the one person whom he had always had faith and confidence to be there for him, love him, and protect him was suddenly holding him down and causing him pain for no discernible reason.

In that moment, Jordan was unable to reconcile his good, kind, loving, and protective mom with the painful circumstances to which he was being subjected. In that moment, Jordan would not have cast his ballot for Robin as Mother of the Year. In that moment, a quick "it's going to be all right," or "this is for your own good," or "someday you'll understand" statement wouldn't have helped at all. Jordan wouldn't have been able to hear it through all the crying and screaming.

This is just a sweet story about a young boy who didn't understand his circumstances. But the truth is, years later, when the stories are not so sweet and we aren't little boys or girls anymore, the pain still feels the same.

When your circumstances are difficult and you can't understand them, they hurt badly. When someone you love dies, it hurts badly. When someone molests you, lies to you, abuses you, or leaves you, it hurts badly. When the worst thing you can imagine becomes a reality in your life, can you even begin to fathom any explanation from God or anyone else that would bring you to a place of contentment? "Oh, so that's why God allowed this to happen to me. Well, now that I have some answers, I'm glad it happened. Thanks for clearing that up for me, Lord. Now I can move on."

I find it impossible to imagine any comforting explanations for the worst circumstances of my life. Sure, maybe I'm glad that something good might eventually come out of my pain or loss, but in the moment, if I were able to choose between learning something from my painful circumstances or not having to experience any pain in the first place, I would choose the latter every single time.

When I was a youth pastor, I received a phone call late one night and learned that two boys in my youth group had been killed in a car accident earlier that evening. I met their parents at the hospital and accompanied them while they identified the bodies.

The next morning, a group of us had gathered at the home of Chris, one of the boys who were killed. I was in the kitchen with Chris's mom, Debbie. We mostly sat in silence. I tried to think of something to say that would offer some comfort, but nothing came to mind. When I tried, Debbie reached across the table, put her hand on mine, and said, "Jim, I know Chris is in heaven. I know he is in a better place. I know he is with Jesus, and he will never again experience pain. I know all that. But, right now, I just want him to walk down those stairs and eat breakfast."

Years later, I can look back and see how Chris's life and death inspired many kids in our church to do great things with their lives and ministries. However, in that kitchen that morning, if I could have explained that to Debbie, she wouldn't have been able to hear it. And if she did, she wouldn't have cared. All she knew was that Chris was gone, and it hurt badly.

Here is the point: if the situations we experience in life are the results of how strong or weak our faith is, then we are all in a lot of trouble. And if our happiness and comfort are based solely on how often we pray, fast, attend church, or refuse to cuss and drink, then why would we need God in the first place?

We cannot equate our painful circumstances with God being bad, weak, or inattentive. On the other hand, we cannot equate our good circumstances with God rewarding us for faithful behavior. Regardless of our faith, sometimes God allows sharks to bite, towers to crumble, and cars to wreck. But while we may never have our moments of pain explained or justified to us, we are still called to trust that God knows what is best for us and will remain by our sides. And having an explanation wouldn't soothe the pain, right?

Many of us have grown up with a skewed definition of faith, so I want to set the record straight. Faith is not a formula that coerces God into doing the things that we desire. Faith is not a magic potion that keeps all of the bad stuff out of our lives. And faith is not a code that, once cracked, explains our circumstances, connects the dots, and makes sense of our pain.

Okay, Jim. We get it. You've been clear about what faith isn't. But you haven't told us what faith is.

Well, that's what I want to discuss in the next chapter.

6

PRAYER, PEOPLE, AND PILLS

So What *Is* Faith?

If faith is not a magic formula devised to trick or trap God into accomplishing our own goals, then what *is* faith?

Put simply, faith is trusting in God's promise to give us more than enough mercy, grace, love, compassion, and strength during our times of most desperate need. Faith is the assurance that, whether our circumstances change for better or worse, we know we are not alone, because God still loves us and he will take care of us.

Too many Christians have been taught a concept of faith that simply isn't true. It's a lie, and the lie sounds like this: "If I have enough faith, God will fix all my problems. And if my problems remain, that is because I don't have enough faith." When you try grasping onto that false concept of faith, you eventually end up losing your faith altogether.

Jesus never promised that if you have enough faith and if you manage to keep an impossibly rigorous religious code, then he will keep all the bad things away. Robin and I have learned the hard way that Jesus never promised to keep the chemicals in your brain balanced so that you don't have to struggle with depression, migraines, or epilepsy.

Jesus *did* make promises, but they sounded more like this:

> In this world you *will* have trouble. But take heart! I have overcome the world. (John 16:33)

> As I was with Moses, so I will be with you; I will *never* leave you nor forsake you. (Joshua 1:5)

> For God so loved the world that he gave his one and only Son, that whoever believes in him *shall not perish* but have eternal life. (John 3:16)

Through these verses, we are promised four things:

1. In this world, we will have trouble.
2. We can have faith that Jesus will help us through the trouble, because he has overcome the world.

3. Jesus will never leave or forsake us.

4. Through faith in Jesus' death and resurrection, we are forgiven by grace.

Most importantly, because of these four promises, when trouble happens, we can lean our lives against something very special:

> Let us then approach God's throne of grace with confidence, so that we may receive mercy and find grace to help us in our time of need. (Hebrews 4:16)

That sums up faith. Faith is trusting that God will take care of you during your most desperate moments. I'm talking about the moments when your heart breaks, you lose the most important person in your life, you're hurt at the most intimate and deepest levels, or you're betrayed by the person you never thought would hurt you. I'm talking about the moments when the tower crumbles and crushes your life.

Whether you hunted the dragon or the dragon hunted you, when the beast tears you to shreds and swallows you whole, what you *want* is for God to change, heal, or fix your circumstances. But what you *need* is to know that you still have access to God and that he will keep his promise to give you enough mercy and grace to survive your next breath. He still loves you, and he promises to take care of you.

This is what Robin experienced on the couch when all she could choke out was a weak groan. Jesus knew exactly what that groan meant, and he answered that prayer with, *I'm here, and I'm not leaving. I will be your strength. I will give you more than enough grace and mercy.*

Mercy is *not* getting what you *do* deserve. In other words, mercy is when you don't get the consequences that should occur if no one intervened on your behalf, the pinnacle of pain that would finish you.

Grace is *getting* what you *don't* deserve and never earned. Grace is when you get to enjoy something you couldn't have achieved on your own.

On a salvation level, mercy is not receiving the deserved condemnation and punishment that are the wages of your sin, and grace is freely receiving forgiveness and righteousness from Jesus—not because you have earned it with a faith formula but because you have put your trust in him.

Asking for grace at God's throne in confidence might mean asking for persistence to take another breath or guidance when you don't know how to take another step. Asking for grace might mean asking for patience when you are fed up with your circumstances, comfort when everything else has failed you, or strength when your knees are about to buckle.

Before continuing, I need to clarify something. There is nothing wrong with asking God to change your circumstances, fix your problems, heal and protect your children, or send you someone with whom you can share your life. In fact, we are commanded to come to our Father and ask for whatever we think we need (Luke 11:9).

As I've already mentioned, if a shark bit my child, I would ask God for healing. If I were in a financial emergency, I would ask God for a solution. If I were struggling in a tough relationship, I would ask God to get involved and change my circumstances.

However, even though this isn't the message we usually want to hear, what I've learned over the course of my life is this:

Sometimes God heals the sick when we ask him to heal the sick. But sometimes he doesn't.

Sometimes God makes checks arrive in the mail. Sometimes he doesn't.

Sometimes God places the person of your dreams right on your front porch. Sometimes he doesn't.

I don't know why God decides to answer one person's prayer in one way and another person's in another way. Maybe that's one of those questions I'll ask when I get to heaven. But I do know that Hebrews 4:16 promises we can boldly and confidently approach our Father God in any and every circumstance because of what Jesus accomplished for us on the cross. And every single time we ask God for help, we can have faith that he will keep his promise to give us the mercy, grace, and strength we need to make it through the day.

We can have confident faith in the promise that God will take care of us in our most desperate times, but most of us still have a few big questions about faith: How will God take care of us in our most desperate times? I understand that God promises to give me grace, mercy, and strength in my time of need, but what will those gifts look like? How do I approach God's throne in confidence? What does that look like practically?

Naturally, I can only speak from my personal experiences, but I want to share three of the many ways God has taken care of Robin and me at times when life hurt so badly that death seemed like a better option than waking up in the morning. Those three things are prayer, people, and pills.

PRAYER

I know it sounds like a religious cliché, but prayer is one of the foundations of our relationship with God. Jesus himself always taught to start with prayer because the very act of praying is an act of faith. Prayer isn't informing God of circumstances he's not aware of so that he can get started on fixing them. God already knows everything that you and I are going through.

When you pray, you make a statement. You acknowledge the fact that you depend on and look toward something higher than yourself in order to make it through the difficult circumstances you are facing. In the movie *Shadowlands*, C. S. Lewis explains prayer: "I pray because I can't help myself. I pray because I'm helpless. I pray because the need flows out of me all the time, waking and sleeping. It doesn't change God, it changes me."[1]

When you pray, you boldly approach the throne of God because you understand that he is the only one who can supply what you truly need, regardless of whether or not your circumstances change at all.

You might be thinking, *I don't know how to pray.* Yes, you do.

A. W. Tozer puts it this way: "The key to prayer is simply praying."[2] Talking to God is all you need to do. Even if the prayer is simply, *Dear God, help me. In Jesus' name, amen.* That's a solid prayer. I've used that one many times.

Pray until you run out of words, and when you run out of words, then lie on your couch or collapse next to your bed and groan. Why? Because prayer is a demonstration of faith. Prayer is the acknowledgment that, in your worst and weakest moments, you understand there is only one person who can help you in the way you need. Only one person has the capability of mercy and the amount of grace that you need. So in faith, you ask, cry, scream, and groan. In faith, you pray.

Some of our favorite verses have pulled Robin and our family through the valley of the shadow of death and depression. One passage comes from Paul in the New Testament, when he begs God to take away what he called his "thorn":

> In order to keep me from becoming conceited, I was given a thorn in my flesh, a messenger of Satan, to torment me. Three times I pleaded with the Lord to take it away from me. But he said to me, "My grace is sufficient for you, for my power is made perfect in weakness." Therefore I will boast all the more gladly about my weaknesses, so that Christ's power may rest on me. That is why, for Christ's sake, I delight in weaknesses, in insults, in hardships, in persecutions, in difficulties. For when I am weak, then I am strong. (2 Corinthians 12:7–10)

Everybody agrees that Paul was not referring to a literal thorn when he asked God to remove the thing in his life that was tormenting him. However, there are many speculations as to what Paul's "thorn" was. Some people say Paul had a physical illness or disability that was tormenting his life. Some think it was blindness or maybe a seizure disorder. Some people have suggested it was a particular struggle or temptation that Paul could not shake or escape despite his deep faith and strong commitment.

I'm glad Paul doesn't tell us what his thorn was, because if he did, then we would be tempted to limit Paul's words to his specific thorn only. Because Paul doesn't tell us the specifics of his circumstances, we can fill in the blanks with whatever is tormenting our lives, whether it's anger, grief, sexual temptation, or physical suffering. Those are all thorns, and they all hurt. We've all asked God to take them away by healing, fixing, or changing them, and the apostle Paul is no different in this regard.

Depression is the thorn that has injured my family the most, but fill in that blank with whatever thorn you have that knocks the wind out of you, puts you in the fetal position, and drives you to your knees at the throne of grace to beg God for the strength you so desperately need. Maybe your thorn is whatever turned you into a dragon. Maybe your thorn is the moment you found out your spouse cheated on you. Maybe your thorn started the morning your kid didn't come downstairs for breakfast. Maybe your thorn began the day the doctor said, "It's not good."

There are two things I want to touch on from Paul's story in 2 Corinthians 12. The first is only my opinion, so you can take it or leave it. In my opinion, when Paul said that he pleaded with the Lord three times to take away the thorn that was tormenting his life, I think Paul pleaded much more than three literal times. If Paul was anything like me, when his thorn was at its worst he prayed and begged God to remove it not three times, but three gazillion times.

The second thing I want to explain from Paul's story is a clarification on translation. When Paul said, "I delight in weaknesses," the word "delight" is not supposed to mean that Paul was like, "Yippee! This is so much fun to be insulted and persecuted!" The feeling we are supposed to gather from this verse is more like, "Just because I can't make sense of what is happening to me, I'm not going to lose my mind. I'm going to remember that God is good and he promises to be here in the middle of this with me. When I feel like I can't make it one more day, Jesus says he'll do it for me."

When all you can do is groan and collapse on the couch, Jesus promises to prop you up. When you are at your weakest, Jesus promises to be your strength. He promises to give you a sufficient amount of grace and mercy to make it through your worst circumstances. You can rest your entire life on those promises. Don't ever forget that.

Through prayer, Paul was reminded that he wasn't alone. He was very aware that, through Christ, he would be sustained, protected, and provided for. In his weaknesses, prayer continually reminded Paul that God would give him the grace, mercy, and strength he desperately needed. Like Paul, we have to keep praying.

PEOPLE

How else does God take care of us in our darkest moments? He uses his people to take care of each other.

One Christmas season at Flatirons, we focused on teaching that before we go out and try to save the world, we should first check on our next-door neighbors to see if they need any help. Jesus taught, "Love your neighbor" (Matthew 22:39), but most of us don't even know our neighbors' names.

After our Saturday night service, a woman in our church named Jodi approached me in the lobby and said, "I'm such a bad neighbor. My neighbors across the street lost their son this past summer to suicide, and I've been meaning to go over and say something, but I haven't yet. Their son did some painting for me this past year, and we had some very nice conversations. Usually their house is covered in Christmas lights, but this year, they don't have a single decoration up. I know they're hurting, but I don't know what to do. I feel horrible that I haven't said or done anything yet. Do you think it's too late to become a better neighbor?"

My response was, "Tell them just that. Stop by and say, 'Hi, I'm from across the street, and I've been meaning to stop by for months, but I've been a bad neighbor. I just wanted to tell you something that your son said to me this past spring when he was working at my house.' Who knows? That could be the best Christmas present they could possibly receive this year."

The next morning, during our Sunday services, I shared the story of talking with Jodi the night before. After the service, a man approached me with tears in his eyes and said, "That was my son. That story you told was about my son. You tell that lady she is more than welcome to come over. We would love to talk to her."

I planned to call Jodi the next day, but this father couldn't wait. He left the church parking lot, drove to Jodi's house, rang her doorbell, and asked, "Do you go to Flatirons?" Jodi immediately knew who this man was. She didn't know that I had shared the story on Sunday morning, but she knew that God had brought him to her door. Tears and hugs followed.

Later, as Jodi sat at the kitchen table with her neighbors, the mother who had lost her son quietly said, "Saturday night, I was begging God for a sign that he was there and he still cared. We went to church the next morning and heard our story being shared from the stage. And now, here we are. God has answered my prayer."

She was absolutely right. God had answered her prayer, and he answered it through his people. God has a rule for his people and his church, and that rule says we are never supposed to attempt to make it through this life alone. This is why God calls his church a body and a new community.

> Carry each other's burdens, and in this way you will fulfill the law of Christ. (Galatians 6:2)

What is "the law of Christ"? His law is to love one another. Jesus said that every word spoken from the prophets and everything God has ever said can be summed up in a single phrase: "Love God and love people." And by "people," Jesus meant everybody. He meant your neighbor, your family, yourself, and even your enemies.

We live in a world where the most overused word in the dictionary is probably *love*. Nearly every song on the radio is about love, what it looks like, how it feels, and what it does to a person. In one conversation—heck, in one sentence—I might use the word *love* several times, yet have it mean several different things: "I love my mom, I love my wife, I love my dog, and I love lasagna." Hopefully I don't love all four of those things in the same way. If I did, that would be pretty sick (although you have no idea how much I actually love lasagna). My question is, when Jesus tells us to love people, what definition of *love* is he looking for?

I'm not going to go over the several Greek definitions

for love. They're often helpful, but I found something I like more. I found a definition of love in the Bible that I believe clearly describes the kind of love we are told to give and receive:

> In this same way, husbands ought to love their wives as their own bodies. He who loves his wife loves himself. After all, no one ever hated their own body, but they feed and care for their body, just as Christ does the church— for we are members of his body. (Ephesians 5:28–30)

Jesus loves us by feeding and caring for us. He feeds us by providing everything in his power to make sure we have the abundant life he intended for us. He cares for us by protecting us from anything that might completely steal, kill, or destroy our lives. We are called to love others in the same way.

So how do we protect and provide for one another? As Galatians 6:2 mentions, I believe we are called to carry one another's burdens.

The best and most effective way to carry one another's burdens is to love unconditionally. Jesus doesn't have any conditions we need to live up to in order to receive his provision and protection. Jesus doesn't tell us to love only the people who prove they are worth loving. Jesus doesn't tell us to love only the people who appreciate your care. Jesus simply says, "As I have loved you, so you must love one another" (John 13:34). If Jesus decided to wait until you or I measured up to a set of conditions that made us worthy, then he would be waiting for a really, really long time. As in, forever.

Jesus says we need to view one another as sick people who need a doctor. It would be ludicrous for a sick person not to act sick, and we need to keep that in mind with those we are called to love. You have to love people when they are ugly, mean, and refuse to love you, appreciate your efforts, or pay you back.

For Robin and me, unconditional love was a hard lesson to learn. To be honest, depressed people aren't much fun sometimes. They cancel plans, break their promises, say mean things, and push away the one thing they need: other people. Sometimes I still have to sift through whether Robin or "depressed Robin" is talking to me, and that's not easy.

In the story Robin shared about herself in chapter 4, I come off as the super husband who took on the house chores and the responsibility of raising the kids. But loving Robin and being a good husband and father are only the results of crawling to the throne of God and receiving a heaping dose of his sufficient mercy and grace. There were times I wanted to give up. There were moments when Robin would say something like, "Everybody's lives would just be easier if I would kill myself," and in the back of my mind, I would think, *I agree. It would be easier if you just went ahead and did it.*

That's not loving or Christlike at all. You're probably thinking, *How awful! You shouldn't have ever felt or thought those things.* You're right. I shouldn't have. But I did. We've all had moments when we find ourselves mulling over unimaginable thoughts and contemplating terrible decisions, and if Jesus hadn't stepped in and taken those thoughts captive (2 Corinthians 10:5), they could have spun out of control.

I'm only trying to be honest and admit that loving unlovable people can be incredibly difficult. We also need to realize that we can be just as unlovable ourselves. Without Jesus and his mercy and grace, none of us is going to make it.

In your darkest, most dragoned moments, you need other people. When you aren't in your darkest moments, you are called to be that person for someone else. So make the phone call, send the card, stop by the house, and love unconditionally.

Meet the needs of those you see hurting. Whether they are depressed, physically ill, or grieving from a death or divorce, hurting people don't typically ask for help. They simply don't have the strength to ask. Instead, they hide in caves. They cocoon themselves in bedrooms with the covers pulled over their heads and the shades pulled down. They don't come out for days or weeks at a time. They are struggling just to survive, just to make it another day.

Carry someone else's burden by doing what needs to be done. Look around your house. The things that need to be done at your place are the same things that need to be done at the house of someone who is hurting. Laundry. Groceries. Cooking. Yard work. Childcare. Do what needs to be done.

While carrying the burden of another is something that Jesus calls us toward, there are two potential dangers of which you should be aware. The first is that, while being broken and at rock-bottom is not a sin, it *is* very fertile soil for sin. It's an easy place for bad habits to take root and grow.

One of the toughest things for me to deal with when Robin was at her worst was trying to figure out if she was choosing not to do something because she was depressed or because she was being selfish and manipulative. There is often a fine line between helping someone and enabling him or her to continue spiraling down into brokenness. I wish there were an exact science or a clear objective rule to apply here, but there isn't. Sometimes you'll get it right. Sometimes you'll get it wrong. And sometimes you'll make it worse.

If you already know what it's like to make a broken person's experience worse, I know how frustrating that can be, and I'm sorry. If you are going to carry the burden of someone who is at rock-bottom, especially someone who is depressed, then you're going to need a safe, godly person who will help carry your burdens. I strongly suggest that this person be a professional counselor or a pastor. I even more strongly suggest that you never share intimate details of your struggles with anyone of the opposite sex, unless, of course, this person is your spouse.

The second potential danger that can come along with attempting to carry someone else's burden is tricking yourself into thinking that you can save the other person.

Let me make myself incredibly clear: *you cannot save anybody.* This is true on a spiritual level, as well as an emotional or physical level. I used to put a lot of pressure on myself as a pastor to come up with a magic phrase, sermon, argument, or application that would cause people to change, but such phrases don't exist. There is no verse I can point to that will fix anybody. There are no twelve-step programs that can fix anybody. You can't un-dragon anybody. Only Jesus can tear someone from the belly of the dragon.

When you carry the burden of another, keep in mind that while cleaning their house and doing their laundry won't lift their spirits forever, those things still need to be done. But don't set yourself up for disappointment by expecting your burden-carrying attempts to fix anyone. There are some things that run so deep on a physical, chemical, emotional, or spiritual level that, if it is ever going to be healed, Jesus himself is going to have to do it.

Our biggest goal should be carrying the burden of a person we love while not standing in the way of the work that only Jesus can do in that person's life. Jesus saves, fixes, and heals. That's his job, not ours. Our job is to love, forgive, protect, pray for, and provide for those who are broken.

There is one last piece I want to mention about carrying the burden of someone who is hurting: stop giving stupid advice.

I'm sorry, but people can say the worst things in the name of trying to help: "You should just try harder. You shouldn't feel like this. Why don't you just think positive, happy thoughts? If you only had more faith, you wouldn't be stuck in this position. If you get out of the house, then you'll feel better. Just pick yourself up by the bootstraps."

Advice offered in ignorance only makes things worse. Try saying something better, something biblical. Remind hurting people about how much they are loved by both you and God. Remind them that the word *failure* is not found anywhere in God's definition of who they are, that God will keep his promise to give them sufficient grace and mercy, and that despite how they feel, he will never leave or forsake them. When everybody else has left for work and school and they are left on the couch, God is there. They are never alone.

PILLS

For my family, God has not only taken care of us through prayer and people, but he has also helped us through (get ready to drop the book and write me a nasty e-mail) pills.

Sometimes God takes care of us through medicine, science, and technology. It is still God taking care of us; he's just using a different outlet. I believe it is time to get rid of the notion that if we only had real faith, then we wouldn't need medication, counseling, doctors, or psychiatrists. Roy Mays was a pastor back in Kentucky who lived years past his cancer diagnosis before finally going home to heaven. I think he said it best: "I don't know which one is making the difference, but we are not going to let up on either one, the prayers or the pills. I will ask the people to keep on praying, and I will keep on popping."[3]

Christians have a list of illnesses and conditions for which they've decided it is acceptable to see a doctor, take a medication, or have a corrective surgery. But when it comes to emotional or mental disorders, they play the all-you-need-is-faith card.

Here's what I think: If you're a diabetic, take the insulin. If you have high blood pressure, lay off the fried foods and take the pills. If you have cancer, go try the chemotherapy. If you're bipolar, take the medication. And if that medication doesn't work, then find another one. Jesus is the only person who can un-dragon your life, but he might choose to do it through science, medicine, or technology. That is completely in line with Scripture.

I once had a youth sponsor who told a high school girl to pray more and stop taking her pills. I fired that youth sponsor in the same way I would have fired that person had they advised the girl to quit praying and take her pills. God works through both, and in the end, he is still the only one who deserves all the credit and glory for healing us and ripping away our scales.

SO WHAT IS FAITH?

Faith understands and embraces the promise that God will never leave or forsake you. Faith acknowledges that, even during your darkest moments, God will keep his promise to provide you with sufficient grace and mercy. Faith means having the ability to approach God's throne of grace in confidence. Faith knows that God will take care of you.

For my wife, Robin, there is no tidy bow on the end of her story. In fact, while writing this chapter, Robin called to tell me she's vomiting at home from another migraine. God may choose never to heal her or set her completely free from the dragons of depression, migraines, and seizures until she leaves this place for her home in heaven. But either way, Robin would remind you of what Jesus said to Paul: "My grace is sufficient for you. When you are weak, I will be your strength" (paraphrased from 2 Corinthians 12:9).

7

MISSING LIMBS, BURNED PIZZA, AND CHREASTER SERVICES

Why Are Some Churches Dragons?

You can pray anywhere you want. You can buy pills at your local pharmacy. But where can you find the people who will support you in your journey toward allowing Jesus to tear away your scales?

Of course, you're supposed to be able to find those people at church because church is supposed to be a community of people who are trying to live out their faith together. But if you're anything like me, the word *church* too often brings a nasty taste to your mouth. For many people, attending a church has been one of the worst experiences of their lives. Why is that?

Why do some churches look like dragons?

WORST FISHING EXPERIENCE EVER

As I've already mentioned, I told God I would only become a pastor if I could talk about real issues in a real way to real people. God was perfectly fine with that deal, but I quickly discovered that many church-attending adults didn't want to hear tough truths. So instead, I spent the first twenty years of my ministry working with high school and college students. They seemed more ready and willing to search for truth, purpose, and a connection to God.

They also helped me understand the importance of constantly creating relevant parables in order to explain deep, unfamiliar spiritual truths in a fresh way. During Jesus' ministry, he told stories about sheep, fishing, and farming because he was surrounded by shepherds, fisherman, and farmers. That makes sense. I, however, was surrounded by suburban, middle-class, iPod-connected, cell-phone-addicted teenagers who were concerned with who was dating who, whose football team was better, and whether or not their skinny jeans made them look fat. (I hate to break it to you, but they did.) Needless to say, I was constantly searching for modern-day object lessons I could use to teach students that God was alive and well in the world and that he had a major plan for their lives if they would choose to follow him.

One spring break, I thought I had landed on the perfect lesson. I was wrong.

The biggest annual event for our high school ministry was called Bible and Beach. We would load up several Greyhound buses, drive all through the night, and arrive in the morning for a week of spring break in the panhandle of Florida. It was kind of like church camp, but instead of hanging out at some lame, tick-infested cabin in the woods, we hung out in the beautiful Gulf of Mexico on the white sands of Panama City Beach. We would wake up, eat breakfast, offer several different Bible studies and seminars, eat lunch, and then spend the rest of the afternoon body surfing, playing beach volleyball, or working on our tans. After dinner, we would have a blowout time of worship and teaching, and then we were off to bed so that we could do it all again the next day. Everybody looked forward to Bible and Beach.

During this particularly fateful Bible and Beach, our youth staff wanted to come up with an event that would get students to consider taking a big step of faith, and I had the perfect idea.

The part of Florida we were going to visit was famous for its deep-sea fishing. (Shark Week won't be playing into this story, but it will be just as gruesome.) There weren't many fishing boat outfits that could accommodate a youth group of our size, so we made the call, placed the reservations, announced the plan to the students, and ended up with nearly 150 people signed up to go deep-sea fishing during free time.

Here was my plan. For the night session after our deep-sea fishing excursion, I would teach about the time when the disciples were caught out in a storm on the lake and they were all afraid of drowning. Then Jesus came walking across the water, and he told Peter to get out of the boat and walk across the waves. Jesus promised he would take care of Peter (Matthew 14:22–32). My application for the teaching would sound something like, "And if Jesus is calling you to do something that you never imagined possible, you need to jump out of the boat and have faith that Jesus will take care of you."

That was the plan.

That's not how things played out.

We arrived at the dock shortly after lunch, checked in, and boarded the fishing boat. All the students took their seats and received a lecture about boat safety, life jackets, and deep-sea fishing dos and don'ts. All was going well.

A few minutes into the voyage, Captain Dave pulled me aside and informed me that he didn't have enough fishing poles for a group as large as ours. But he said there was another ship close to where we were headed that could provide us with some more fishing poles. I told Captain Dave that the plan sounded great.

We soon spotted another ship with a deckhand who was waving and holding a ton of fishing poles. Captain Dave began maneuvering our boat toward the other. As soon as we were close enough to make the trade, one of our deckhands leaned over the edge to grab the extra fishing poles. But just as he reached out, a weird wave rolled underneath the boats that caused our boat to move up and their boat to move down. Our deckhand's arm got caught between the boats, and when they collided, they . . . *cut his arm off!*

They didn't just break his arm. They didn't just cut his arm. They cut his arm *off.* His arm landed on our deck in front of 150 kids who sat in their benches watching the whole thing like some bloody, chainsaw-killer horror movie.

There was a collective gasp that was soon followed by screaming, crying, vomiting, and fainting. Everybody looked at me, waiting for me to do something, but what was I going to do? If I had thought of it at the time, I would have yelled, "All hands on deck!" Admit it: that would have been hilarious, even if completely insensitive. (I never said I was perfect.)

Instead, in the moment, I was frozen and dumbfounded.

One of the other boat crewmen picked up the guy's arm and stuck it in an ice chest. It was such a hectic few minutes that I don't even remember what they did with the injured man. I just remember that Captain Dave turned the boat around, and we headed back to the dock. Our fishing trip was over. Correction: our fishing trip was an absolute disaster.

As the students jumped off the boat back at the pier, I could overhear their conversations: "That was the worst thing I've ever experienced . . . I am never doing anything like that again . . . How could Jim put us through something like this?"

On top of all that, my sermon application for that night was ruined. I knew that if I stood in front of those students and told them they could trust Jesus enough to jump out of the boat, I would find 150 faces staring up at me, all saying the same thing: "Forget that! I don't think I'm ever getting on a boat again, and if I do, I'm definitely not going near the edge."

At the end of the week, when the buses arrived home, nobody ran to their parents and said, "Oh, Mom! My faith is so much deeper because of this trip. Worship was incredible. The teaching was profound." In fact, no one even mentioned Jesus. The only thing you could hear students telling their parents was, "We went fishing and some dude got his arm cut off. It was horrible. Worst experience ever."

WORST CHURCH EXPERIENCE EVER

While my fishing-trip metaphor completely fell apart for those students on the beach, it stands as a perfect metaphor for what many of us have found at church: an absolute disaster. You psyched up the guts to jump onto the boat, but something horrific happened, and you decided never to jump onto that boat again.

When I meet new people in our church lobby on weekends, one of the most frequent conversations I have starts the same way: "I haven't been to church in a long time."

I used to ask why, but now I pretty much know the answer. It's seldom, "I disagree with the Bible" or, "I don't like Jesus." As a matter of fact, in all my travels throughout the world, including Muslim countries like Afghanistan or Hindu areas of India, I have yet to meet someone who says, "I just don't like that Jesus guy." There are people who don't believe Jesus is who he claimed to be. There are people who struggle with what Jesus claimed to be true. But I've never met anyone who struggled with Jesus because he was too loving, kind, forgiving, and compassionate.

Instead, when people say, "I haven't been to church in a long time," they usually follow it with, "because something horrible happened. Somebody really hurt me at church. After that, I swore I'd never go back."

They usually sound like a bunch of high school students

describing the worst spring break experience of their lives: "My life was a mess. I was searching for something better. I was searching for truth and a better way. My friends invited me to come to church. They said it would help. Eventually I was so lost and hopeless that I decided to give it a try. I got onboard, but what followed was one of the most painful experiences of my life. When it was over, I walked away and never looked back."

In short, they risked going near the edge, and it cut them to pieces.

After hearing so many of these stories, when people begin talking to me about how they haven't been to church in a long time, my typical response is, "I don't blame you. I had to become the pastor of a church in order to find one I wanted to go to."

That response usually gets a few weird looks, but it's true. I'm not saying that the church I pastor is better than any other church. We have our own problems and challenges.

But we *are* trying to build a church community that doesn't shy away from what Jesus said is a better, truer, more abundant way to live. We've committed ourselves to not being hurtful, mean, or condemning. We've committed ourselves to offering biblical hope, help, directions, and solutions for a better way to live life. We've thrown away boring, impossible, impractical, unhelpful, and untrue teaching, and we talk about real things in real ways to real people who have real problems. We refuse to shy away from the messy stuff, because that's where life happens.

In short, we've decided not to become the "worst church experience ever."

A few years ago, I remember being excited to hear a particular Christian speaker who was supposed to be really good. I finally had an opportunity to hear him in person, and I was pumped. I brought my pen and paper, and I was ready to take notes. (In preacher language, that means I was ready to write down anything worth plagiarizing.)

Yet his opening lines quickly disappointed me. He said, "I want to talk to you about how life can be hard sometimes. For example, my wife and I just moved into a brand-new house, but we can't quite get the new oven figured out. When my wife makes homemade pizza, the crust gets burned before the cheese even melts. Our traditional Friday Pizza Night is ruined. But that's life sometimes, right?"

After working with the multitude of lost, broken, and jacked-up people who have walked through the doors of Flatirons over the years, I know I might be oversensitive in this area, but come on. Seriously? You want to talk about how life can be hard, but your opening point of connection is, "The hardest thing in my life is that the oven at my house doesn't measure up to my personal standards"?

I don't care about the median income of your church, where your church is located, or what denomination you are or aren't affiliated with. I don't care whether your community is comprised of hip twentysomethings or if you meet in the geriatric ward of a nursing home. None of those factors changes the simple truth that every room is full of people who are wrestling with issues more devastating than, "Excuse me, dear, but this isn't how I like my pizza."

What about the man in the audience who is thinking, *So your wife is a bad baker? I'm sorry. My wife is sleeping with her boss and doesn't think I know about it yet. So shut up and eat your burned pizza.*

What about the single mom who is thinking, *At least you have food. I came in here to say a prayer because I don't know how I'm going to afford the groceries to feed my family tomorrow?*

What about the lady in the seat two rows in front of me who wears sunglasses indoors during an evening service to cover up her swollen black eye? What does a faulty oven have to do with the tears running down her bruised cheek?

Or what about my wife, who has dealt with over thirty years of migraine headaches, epileptic seizures, and the bipolar disorder that has ruthlessly tried to rob her of all joy, happiness, and health? What about her? To be honest, as soon as the speaker gave his opening connection point, I turned to my friend and said, "This is where Robin would stand up, yell something that nice Christian girls shouldn't yell, and walk out."

Eventually the lady in the sunglasses walked out early. So did we.

To be fair, maybe the sermon took a sharp, drastic turn for the better after we left. But even if it did, most of the people sitting in my section had already tuned out or left the building because the message seemed irrelevant and unhelpful.

Sometimes I'm amazed that people still choose to try church anymore. People all over the world gather the courage to walk through the church doors because they are searching for a connection to purpose, truth, and a better life. Jesus said:

> I am the way and the truth and the life. No one comes
> to the Father except through me. (John 14:6)

Everything that we are searching for can be found in and through Jesus, and if Christians are being set free from their dragons, then we should be able to find what we're searching for in the church. The dilemma is that finding Jesus in church is often hard to do.

So why does attending church so often become a person's worst experience ever?

A HOSPITAL FOR DRAGONS

A few years ago, I drove my dad to the eye doctor so he could have laser surgery in order to remove a cataract. On our way home from the hospital, we stopped at a restaurant for some lunch. I don't remember how the conversation started, but about halfway through the meal, I looked at my dad and said, "You know what? I don't know much of anything about your side of the family, your childhood, or how you were raised. I don't even know how you became a Christian."

For the next two hours, he poured out his story, and I discovered a whole new side of my dad. He told me about growing up in poverty and living in small houses and shacks. One time, his family lived in the chicken house on a farm because that was all they could afford.

As my dad continued to reflect on his past, I could see in his eyes that he was reliving some of those awful moments. He told me about his abusive, alcoholic father. One time, his father violently beat him with a horse harness out in the fields until my dad escaped. He told me about the anger and hatred he felt toward his father.

He told me about finding the family and structure he desperately needed after joining the army. He shared his journey of faith. He was on the deck of a ship headed for Korea when he contemplated committing suicide by throwing himself overboard because he felt so alone. In that moment, as he asked God why he felt so abandoned, he suddenly received a sense of peace he had never felt before. He realized God had always been with him, through the good times as well as the bad times. That night, he surrendered his life to Jesus.

While we ate lunch that day, he told me stories I had never heard before. I began to see my dad not just as my father but also as a man who had struggled and wrestled with life and God. He was a man who never stopped fighting to become a better person.

About a year before my dad passed away, I brought up that conversation about his past, and I asked him if he remembered that talk. His response floored me. He said, "You know, even though I've spent my whole life being a minister, I've always felt like a hypocrite."

"Why?" I asked.

He answered, "I stood in front of people and told them they should forgive their enemies, but I've still never forgiven my dad for the pain he caused in my life."

After a few minutes of silence, I looked at my dad and said, "That's why you were such a great minister. People related to you because you truly understood how hard it is to forgive."

I don't think he completely believed me, so I had him share his story via video for all of Flatirons. At the end of each of those weekend services, following standing ovations, my dad closed the service from the stage in prayer. In the lobby that weekend, countless men and women, both young and old, who had lived through similar experiences lined up to tell my dad, "Thank you. Me too. Now I know I'm not alone. There's someone else who understands what I've walked through."

According to my mom, sharing his story of faith and his struggles with forgiveness was one of the most healing moments in my dad's life. According to the response from the community at Flatirons, it was also one of the most healing moments for hundreds, maybe even thousands, of people struggling with the same issues in Colorado.

Why was telling his story so healing for my dad and for Flatirons?

Because my dad was willing to admit he was just as screwed up as everyone else. He didn't pretend to be completely cured from the sin in his life. Instead, he shared his story without omitting the messy parts, and that allowed everyone at Flatirons to take a deep breath.

Some churches claim that you have to be free from your dragons before you can walk through the doors, but that's not what Jesus intended for his church. Remember, the number one question asked of Jesus had nothing to do with theology, doctrine, or rules. It was, "Why are you friends with people like that? Why do you eat dinner and associate with sinners? Why do you spend time with the lost, broken outcasts of the world?"

"Jesus, why do you hang out with dragons?"

Jesus knew exactly why he came to earth and what he wanted to accomplish. To communicate both his mission and also his followers' marching orders for the future, Jesus described his church as a hospital for sick and wounded people.

> As Jesus went on from there, he saw a man named Matthew sitting at the tax collector's booth. "Follow me," he told him, and Matthew got up and followed him.
>
> While Jesus was having dinner at Matthew's house, many tax collectors and sinners came and ate with him and his disciples. When the Pharisees saw this, they asked his disciples, "Why does your teacher eat with tax collectors and sinners?"
>
> On hearing this, Jesus said, "It is not the healthy who need a doctor, but the sick. But go and learn what this means: 'I desire mercy, not sacrifice.' For I have not come to call the righteous, but sinners." (Matthew 9:9–13)

Matthew, the guy who wrote one of the four gospels, was on the Most Likely to Be Picked Last by Jesus list created by the religious people.

I'm sure that Matthew didn't need any religious quacks to tell him that God had every reason to be angry with him and that he didn't deserve to be spending any time with Jesus. Matthew already knew the terrible things he had done throughout life. He wasn't hanging out with Jesus because he felt worthy of his company. Matthew was hanging out with Jesus because Jesus had invited him. Jesus knew that Matthew needed mercy, not religious lectures and laws.

When Matthew heard Jesus compare his church to a hospital for sick people, Matthew immediately wanted in. He knew he was sick. He knew he was a mess. He knew parts of his life were messed up, screwed up, jacked up, and every other type of up there is, and that's why he was hanging out with Jesus. Because only sick people need doctors.

Can you imagine if you were to have a terrible accident and end up cutting your arm off today? Can you imagine doing your best to stop the bleeding and then rushing to the emergency room only to be greeted by a group of hospital screeners who tell you, "I'm sorry, but you just can't be here. It seems you've cut your arm off. You're covered in blood and smelly filth, and we're afraid you will make the other patients feel uncomfortable"?

Can you imagine holding your dying child in your arms but being told at the hospital doors that because of your kid's particular disease, you aren't allowed in the hospital? Well, that's how a lot of people feel when they come to church. If you're told enough times that you aren't good enough to be there, then eventually you will begin to believe those lies. You will decide to try again when you're less sick, but the truth is that you'll never come back because you'll never get better. Jesus, the only person who could have healed you and fixed your problems, was never given the chance. It's not his fault, and it's not your fault. It's the church's fault.

CHREASTER SERVICES

A few years ago, I was talking to a young lady in our church named Karen, and she told me about bringing her boyfriend to Flatirons for Easter weekend. Karen had been dating Mike for several months, but despite her multiple attempts to invite him to church, Mike continually refused.

Mike was in the military. In fact, he was in one of those special operations branches that deploy people to faraway places in the world for two or three weeks, and then send them back home under strict orders to keep their missions top secret. In short, Mike was a tough guy. If I were to reveal any more than that, I'm pretty sure that upon publication of this book, several blacked-out SUVs would pull up to my house, take me away, and I'd be forced to eat Cuban food for the foreseeable future.

Anyway, when I asked Karen why Mike wouldn't come

to church, she replied, "Mike has seen and done some rough stuff. He doesn't think he should be allowed in church. He's convinced God hates him, and he thinks the roof will collapse on top of him if he walks through the doors."

After months of repeated attempts, Karen finally talked Mike into coming to Flatirons for one of our Easter services. They sat as far back and as close to the exit as possible in order to escape the pieces of roof that Mike believed were bound to come showering down.

I should quickly explain that Flatirons does Easter differently than other churches. We get a lot of Chreasters. A Chreaster is someone who only attends church twice a year: Christmas and Easter. (For the record, Chreasters gave themselves that name, not me.) This usually means that the moment their parents gave them the option not to attend church anymore, they were out. Chreasters are, however, willing to keep Mom happy and wax nostalgic by showing up to church twice a year.

So during Easter and Christmas, recognizing the fact that we'll be lucky enough to have a bunch of Chreasters through the doors, I always try to do three things with my teachings. First, I make sure that I'm not teaching the same thing they heard last year. Second, I make sure the teaching is relevant to real life and difficult issues. And third, I tie in the birth, death, and resurrection of Jesus.

On the Easter weekend that Mike finally came to church

with Karen, I taught on David and Bathsheba, because nothing screams "Easter" like playing rooftop Peeping Tom, committing adultery, throwing wild drinking parties, and murdering an innocent man (2 Samuel 11–22). You should read the whole story sometime.

My emphasis in the teaching was on the prophet Nathan's confrontation with David about David's sin. In the story, David had just slept with a married woman, murdered her husband, and then taken her as his wife in order to cover up the fact that she was carrying his illegitimate baby. Nathan confronted David with his sin by telling a fictional story about a rich man who stole a poor man's only sheep because he didn't want to eat any of his own flock. Not catching on to the illustration, David interrupted the story with his idea for the rich man's punishment:

> David burned with anger against the man and said to Nathan, "As surely as the LORD lives, the man who did this must die! He must pay for that lamb four times over, because he did such a thing and had no pity." (2 Samuel 12:5–6)

David told Nathan that he thought it was impossible for the rich man to ever right the wrong he had committed. If it were up to David, he would have killed the sheep thief.

At this point during Easter service, Mike was leaning

forward in his chair with fists clenched. He was ready to join David in giving the sheep thief exactly what he deserved. But the next verse hit too close to home:

Then Nathan said to David, "You are the man!" (2 Samuel 12:7)

At this, Mike leaned back in his chair. As Nathan reminded David of all the ways God had taken care of him and all the things that David had done wrong, Karen could see the weight of Mike's history crushing him into the chair. Surely, the ceiling was soon to collapse. Mike began planning his exit strategy as I continued reading:

Then David said to Nathan, "I have sinned against the LORD."

Nathan replied, "The LORD has taken away your sin. You are not going to die." (2 Samuel 12:13)

At this verse, Mike snapped his head over to Karen and asked, "Is that true? Is it possible for people like David and me to be forgiven?"

With tears, Mike waited for Karen to say, "No. Not someone like you," but instead Karen looked him in the eyes and told him the truth: "Yes. It's possible. That's why I wanted you here today."

That is the message of Easter. That is the message of Jesus, and it should be the message of his church. The message is this: everyone is a dragon (Romans 3:23), and the price for being a dragon is condemnation and death (Romans 6:23), but regardless of what you've done to become a dragon (Romans 3:23), Jesus wants to forgive you and slay your dragon (John 3:16).

Mike didn't come to church to be told he was a dragon. He already knew that. Every time he looked in the mirror, he saw a monster staring back at him. He didn't come to church to be told he was a sinner or to be reminded of his mistakes. He lived with them every day.

When David confessed his sin, he didn't receive what he deserved. He received grace and mercy in his time of need. There were still plenty of repercussions on David and those around him from his mistakes. Nathan didn't promise David that God would clean up his mess and everyone could pretend like it had never happened. He told David that, in spite of his past, God still loved him and wanted to be a part of his life. His life wasn't over. He didn't have to let his past condemn his future. Grace and hope were his.

Mike looked at the life of David and concluded that, if David was able to receive grace, mercy, hope, and love from God, then maybe he had a chance as well. What blew Mike away was the fact that he could quit worrying about the possibility of the ceiling collapsing and instead focus on the fact that God wanted to extend grace, mercy, and forgiveness to him.

The message of Jesus is this: "Yes, Mike. You are exactly why I came here and did what I did. I want to un-dragon you." The message of Jesus' church must sound the same. The dilemma is that before many of us can even get the chance to bump into Jesus and listen to his message, we're pushed away by all of the weird, religious nonsense that too many churches shove down our throats.

We are often turned away from church before we can ask the important questions: "Am I welcome here? Is it okay for someone like me to be here when I'm not yet sure that everything you're saying is true? Am I alone in my problems or does anyone else understand? Can the teachings of Jesus apply to my life? Can he actually move me toward better experiences and circumstances? Is the life that Jesus describes even possible for me anymore?"

We are all open to something better. What man doesn't want to become a better husband, father, son, or friend? What woman doesn't want to become a better wife, mother, daughter, or friend? Who doesn't wish that he had made better decisions, cared better for those around him, kept his promises more often, and disappointed himself and others less?

We all want something better, but due to our past

experiences with church, many of us think, *If the people sitting around me in church knew the stuff I've done in the past and the stuff I'm currently involved in, they'd stop the service. Some men in suits would come to my row, pull me from my chair, show me the door, and tell me not to come back until I've sorted out my life.*

There are too many churches that stand in the way of people connecting with Jesus because they put off the vibe that you need to have your life together before you can walk through the doors. There are too many churches that relish in telling people they're sinners. People don't *go* to church *for* that. People *come* to church *with* that. We already know the truth about ourselves. What we are looking for is hope and the possibility of grace. To quote the great Lloyd Christmas from *Dumb and Dumber*, we want to walk in the doors of a church and exclaim, "So . . . you're saying there's a chance?!"[1]

Every one of us has been a dragon. Lucky for us, Jesus came for dragons, and what he wants more than anything is to have them welcomed into his church.

Now we know why some churches are dragons, but how do we change that?

8

GAY GUYS, GANGSTERS, AND EVERYONE ELSE

A Challenge to Fight for Your Church

I was headed to my annual doctor's checkup in order to get another year's worth of refills for my ADHD medication. Trust me, I didn't want to miss that appointment.

On the day of my appointment, my regular doctor turned out to be sick. (That was not reassuring.) The receptionist asked if I would be comfortable with another doctor in the same practice who was a woman. Since my visit had nothing to do with the general swimsuit area, I said that was fine. As I was waiting in the examination room, reading the same magazines from last year, the doctor finally walked in. We went through the typical introductory pleasantries, then she sat on a stool, flipped open her laptop, and began studying the screen as she occasionally asked me questions about my medical history. Eventually she asked, "Mr. Burgen, what is it that you do?"

This question has always made me uneasy. Not because I'm ashamed of my profession as a pastor, but because people's responses to my answer are often unusual. At parties, "I'm a pastor" usually causes people to hide their drinks behind their backs, turn down the music, and begin rapidly spreading the word: "The bald guy's religious. Watch out."

On airplanes, "I'm a pastor" usually causes those next to me to either hide what they're reading for the next four hours or enter into a lecture on why they don't believe in organized religion. Their defenses often range from the creation-versus-evolution debate to the Crusades of the Middle Ages.

So when the doctor asked what I did for a living, I took a deep breath and said, "I'm a pastor." She didn't flinch, which was a good sign. Instead she asked which church I worked for. I told her I worked at Flatirons, and she replied, "That big one?"

After I confirmed that our church, indeed, was "that big one," she said, "Oh, I love your church. I invite people to go there all the time."

"Awesome! How long have you been coming?" I responded.

"Oh, I've never been there myself. I'm a member somewhere else, but I could never invite anyone to come to my church, so I send them to yours."

Wow, I thought. How sad would it be to know people who are walking through a dark time, know that Jesus is the only person who could ever help them, but also know that you could never invite them to your own church because you wouldn't be sure they could find Jesus there?

This brings me to my challenge.

It is incredibly easy to church-bash and point out everything that is wrong in everyone else's church. I've done my fair share of church-bashing over the years. However, as I look back on my life, I realize I'm also guilty of doing almost everything that I bash other churches for doing. I wish it weren't true, but it is.

While there is no shortage of things to be critical of in today's church, the truth is that, as Christians, we shouldn't be fighting *against* the church. We should be fighting *for* the church. The church is the bride of Christ and Jesus' primary instrument in prevailing over the gates of hell (Matthew 16:18). So let's begin fighting for the church, not against it.

After all, Jesus wants to take church out of the dragon too.

If dragons cannot comfortably walk into your church building and have genuine, nonjudgmental, truth-filled conversations with the people in your church, then where else in the world can they find the un-dragoning love of Jesus?

Church should be a place where everyone is welcome and has the chance to bump into Jesus. Many of you, upon reading this, may be experiencing some mixed emotions. If you've ever been the victim of a church where hardly anyone seems welcome, then you're probably thinking, *I wish I could find a church like that.*

If that's your story, then keep looking. I promise those kinds of churches are out there. There aren't many. But if you keep looking, you'll find one, and it will be more than worth it.

But others of you might already have a church home and be nodding in agreement with me, thinking, *I want my church to look more like that.* It's to you that I offer a challenge. Why don't you become instrumental in revitalizing your church and transforming it into the inviting, loving community that Jesus intended?

Now, before you jump out of your chair in excitement and determination, I have a word of warning: be careful what you ask for. If you pursue a life like the one Jesus demonstrated, one where you join with others and become a church that is truly a hospital for sick people, then guess what? Sick people show up. In my experience, a lot of them show up.

And that's not all. Not only will sick people show up to churches that are genuinely running after Jesus, but guess what they'll do when they get there? They will act sick. News flash: dragons act like dragons. It's not rocket science.

So if you think you're up for the challenge, then instead of panicking on the back end, let's prepare on the front end for how to respond when dragons enter your church and start torching the place.

In this chapter, I'm going to offer a few "what would you do in this case?" scenarios. Some of you may think that I'm throwing out extreme or rare examples of sick people in the hospital of Flatirons, but they are normal, weekly occurrences. I want you to be thinking about how you and your church would handle the following scenarios, and then measure it up to the way you see Jesus handling these situations in the Bible.

If you read these stories and *still* feel committed to the challenge of transforming your church into a genuine hospital for dragons, then in the next chapter we'll discuss some small, practical steps you can begin taking.

AN ODD BATHROOM BREAK

I was in the men's room, standing at a urinal between services at Flatirons, which was quite an accomplishment. Until we moved into a bigger building, we were running six weekend services with only four urinals to accommodate the several thousand men who had just downed several thousand cups of coffee. Anyway, I was standing there when out of the stall emerged a rather large man. I heard a slight gasp followed by, "Pastor Jim? Is that you?"

The timing seemed a bit awkward, but I confirmed I was Pastor Jim. For the record, I hate the title Pastor Jim, but I've surrendered my opposition only because I think it makes people feel more comfortable when they talk to me. I think it's kind of like when I go to the doctor, and I want the person who is about to stick things in my ears and shove a flashlight down my throat to be much more than my buddy Dan. "Buddy Dan" can't do those things. "Doctor Phillips" can.

Anyway, the voice continued, "Oh, wow. I was praying that I would get to meet you. God has been changing my life. Since I've been coming to Flatirons, God has delivered me from my addiction to gay porn and all kinds of other weird sexual stuff."

Did I mention that I was taking a leak in the men's room?

I zipped up, turned around, and standing in front of me was a three-hundred-pound man with frost-tipped hair, rainbow-colored suspenders, an unbuttoned shirt, and several gold chains. Before I could head to the sink to wash my hands, he reached toward me and said, "My name's Richard. Can I have a hug?"

I didn't have time to respond. Before I knew it, my face was buried in chest hair and gold chains as Richard swayed back and forth, repeating, "Thank you, Pastor Jim. Praise Jesus."

A few thoughts were running through my mind. First, if I hadn't yet had time to wash my hands, then I *knew* Richard hadn't. Second, stuff like that never used to happen at my old church. Third, he was wearing nice cologne, and I was wondering where he bought it.

I was soon able to pry myself from Richard's embrace, wash up, and continue our conversation in the lobby. I set up an appointment for Richard to tell me more of his story (in a setting other than a bathroom), which we eventually put on video and shared with our entire church.

Richard's story was a story of sexual abuse as a child from both his father and his former youth minister. It was a story of addiction to pornography and of a kid running away to seek protection in Christian rescue centers and being turned away time and time again. It was a story of hearing voices, of attempting suicide, of meeting Jesus in a dream, and of being kicked out of churches that claimed to stand for the same principles that Jesus did.

It was also a story of Richard and his partner, Gary, being invited by their waitress to Flatirons one weekend. That weekend I preached on the story of the prodigal son. Coincidentally, I also told the story about the monkeys that ended up in filthy cages covered in their own waste but who were eventually rescued. I taught that, in the same way, Jesus wants to rescue us, wash us clean, love us, and set us free.

That was the first time Richard had ever heard about real grace. A few months later, Richard was baptized in a lake. After his baptism, he came up to me on the beach and said, "Pastor Jim, I have a question. I have a date tonight. With a girl. Do you think Jesus would be okay with us having a glass of wine?"

I gave Richard a big hug and said, "Yeah, Richard. If you're careful, I think Jesus would be okay with that."

For the record, I wish I could tell you that Richard had a perfect date and met the woman of his dreams, but the truth is that the date went terribly. I wish I could tell you that from the moment Richard met Jesus, he never thought about or struggled with the voices of homosexuality or depression ever again, but it's not true. Richard struggled and failed repeatedly over the years, but he did it with the assurance of God's love and grace.

A few years after meeting Richard in that men's room, I was informed that Richard had died alone in a hotel room from a heart attack. However, I knew the true story. I knew that Richard died in a hotel room with Jesus in his heart and right by his side. Now Richard is home with Jesus. He's not home because he always did what was best and true. He's home because of what Jesus accomplished for him.

Could you be friends with Richard? Could Richard come and eat dinner at your house? If Richard came to your church, whether he began to change or nothing ever changed, would he be able to call your church his home? How would you respond to the many people who would ask you, "Why do you hang out with people like Richard?"

TATTOO TONY

Flatirons was hosting an event for all of the men in our church on a Sunday night after the Broncos game. I got there a few minutes early, and as I was walking through the lobby, a voice called out, "Hey, Pastor Jim. Got a minute?"

That's how I met Tony. Every exposed inch of Tony's flesh was covered in cheap, bad tattoos—the kind you get in prison, not at a $150/hour tattoo shop. I learned from Tony that he was in his thirties and had just finished a twenty-year prison sentence. He had only been out for a few months, and he had been coming to Flatirons for the last few weeks. He said, "I want to tell you something cool. I haven't been high in thirty days. Nothing. No drugs. No alcohol. Nothing."

I told him I thought that was awesome. Then he said, "You know those orange-and-white stickers of the Flatirons logo that people put on their cars? Well, the other night, I really needed some help and I was praying,

Come on, God. I need you to help me. If you don't do something, I'm going to go get high. Please do something. I was starting to get really mad at God because I was praying, but he wasn't doing anything.

"So I got in my car, and headed toward the next town over because that's a good place to buy. I was driving down the road, praying, *Come on, God. Do something!* Right at that moment, a car cut in front of me in traffic. I was about to flip them off, but I saw they had a Flatirons sticker on their car. For some reason, that was enough. I was like, 'All right, God. I get it.' I turned my car around, went home, and I didn't get high that night."

I was laughing with him on the couch, but then he turned very serious and asked, "Hey. Do you really think God forgives *everything*?"

"Yeah, Tony. I really do," I replied.

"But I've done some really bad stuff. When I was in prison, I was part of a gang." He then told me the name of the gang, which I will not mention because they are still alive and well and working both inside and outside the prison systems of Colorado. When I mentioned the name of this gang to some cop friends of mine, they turned pale.

Tony continued, "Jim, these are some bad guys. They're the kind of guys that will break into your house and kill your wife and kids. People are dead because of me. Families have been destroyed because of me. Even if it's true that

God forgives me, I think about what I've done all the time, and I don't think I can forgive myself."

I sat there on that couch looking into the eyes of a man who had once stood for every hateful thing I could ever imagine. I couldn't help but think that if he had hurt or murdered one of my family members, I didn't know what I would do. Yet I was also looking into the tear-filled eyes of a man who was waiting for me to tell him whether Jesus loved him or hated him.

I told Tony that his story reminded me of another racist murderer named Saul, who had to change his name to Paul in a New Testament version of the witness protection program. I told Tony that Paul became a man who, other than Jesus himself, was responsible for more people following Christ than probably anyone else in history.

I told Tony that God loved him and Jesus died for him. I told him that he was already forgiven, and with Jesus' help, Tony might someday be able to forgive himself.

Could you become friends with Tony? If Tony were your son, brother, or husband, what would you have told him? I'm not asking what you think Tony deserves. That's an easy answer. He deserves what every other sinner on this planet deserves. That includes you and me.

Instead, I'm wondering what Tony would find if he were to come to your church in an attempt to bump into Jesus.

JESSICA'S JOURNEY

One weekend in the lobby, I was informed that someone named Jessica was looking for me. When I saw her waiting in line to talk with me, I knew it was Jessica even though we had never met. As she reached out her hand to shake mine, she said, "My name is Jessica. I'm an eight-year, postoperative transgender. I have two questions. First, am I welcome here? Second, if I meet a man and fall in love a few years from now, would you be willing to do my wedding?"

In case anyone missed it, let me review the scenario that was playing out in the lobby. Jessica, an overweight, six-foot-tall woman, used to be a man named Jeff eight years prior. She wanted to know if she could stay at Flatirons, and she also wanted to know whether or not I would speak at her hypothetical wedding to a man sometime in the future.

To be fair, if I hadn't already been prepared for my encounter with Jessica, I think I would have found myself speechless. But she had already made the rounds around church using this peculiar introduction until someone finally said, "I think you should just talk to Pastor Jim himself." The news made it to me before Jessica did. I had given her situation a little thought, but I wondered how well I would handle it when the time came. What would I think? What would she say? How would I respond?

I took a deep breath, and said, "Jessica, as far as the

wedding goes, I would never promise anybody that I would do their hypothetical wedding years from now. Let's deal with that scenario when and if it ever comes up. Here is what I *do* know. I don't understand what you've been through. I don't understand your journey or what has brought you to your current circumstances. But I *do* know that God loves you. The Bible is clear about that. I also know that Jesus died for your sins and mine. The Bible is clear about that too. The Bible is also clear that because God loves you, so does his church and so do I. You're more than welcome to be here."

She soon followed that response with another question: "Can I join a women's Bible study?"

I replied, "I don't know. This is all new territory for me. I've never worked through anything like this before, so I don't know yet. But if you can be patient with us, we'll figure it out together. I know that we won't do it perfectly, and we will both make mistakes along the way. But I know for a fact that God loves you, and you are welcome here. We can figure the rest out together."

Over the next several months, Jessica sat on the front row, taking notes on every single sermon. (In fact, she still does.) But eventually her transgender community kicked her out because she began going to "that church" that teaches homosexual behavior is outside of God's best plan for anyone's life.

Recently Jessica signed up to attend our women's retreat. Through my conversations with Jessica, I am convinced she is looking for God's truth in her life. She also knows that the elders, staff, and I cannot see how the physiology of her body and God's truth for her life line up with one another. She also knows that she gets to attend and serve at the retreat, but she has agreed to sleep in separate quarters.

I know that people on both sides of this argument probably have issues with how I've handled this situation. I get it. If I were you, maybe I'd have a problem with me as well. But what else do you want me to do? Should I have told her she made a mistake? Should I have stoned her to death? Should I have insisted that she have a reversal surgery before she can come back? Jessica's biggest problems cannot be corrected by another surgery. But maybe in a place like Flatirons, they can be healed by Jesus.

Hopefully we already understand that there are some things in life that are so deep, vast, difficult, and complicated that, if anything is ever going to heal, then the power of the Holy Spirit of Jesus Christ himself is going to have to do all the work. That level of healing is above everyone else's pay grade. If that is true, where does Jessica have the best chance of experiencing God's presence and life-changing truth? Can Jessica bump into Jesus at your church?

Before you answer that question, let's look at a story found in Luke 5 about a guy named Simon Peter.

A GOOD CATCH

Jesus had been teaching to a growing number of people on the shore of a lake. As the crowd grew, it became difficult to see or hear Jesus, so he decided to paddle a boat a few feet from the shore so that he could communicate better. Jesus borrowed the boat from a local fisherman named Simon Peter.

When the time of teaching was over, Jesus told Peter to paddle out a little farther and put down his fishing nets so they could catch some fish. Peter's response was actually an argument. I don't blame him. Think about it. Peter had been fishing all his life. He knew what worked and what didn't. Suddenly some construction-worker-turned-preacher wanted to tell him how to do his job. In that part of the world, you fished at night, but it was the middle of the day when Jesus told Peter to drop his nets. So Peter argued:

> Simon answered, "Master, we've worked hard all night and haven't caught anything. But because you say so, I will let down the nets." (Luke 5:5)

Peter argued but then agreed to let down his nets.

Why? I wonder what was going on in Peter's world that caused him to say, "What the heck? I'll give it a try." Maybe it was because, on that day, everything Peter knew about fishing had left him with absolutely no fish. Peter said they had worked hard all night but hadn't caught anything. No fish means no money. And no money means no food on the table for Peter. My guess is that if Peter already had a boatful of fish, he probably wouldn't have agreed to fish in the middle of the day.

In other words, Peter had done everything he knew to do, but nothing was working. At that point, he was open to other suggestions, including those from a carpenter.

When they had done so, they caught such a large number of fish that their nets began to break. So they signaled their partners in the other boat to come and help them, and they came and filled both boats so full that they began to sink. (Luke 5:6–7)

During a desperate moment in his life, Peter decided to take a gamble and listen to what Jesus said was a better way to fish. He tried it, and it worked. In fact, it worked better than he could have ever expected.

But Peter's response was not, "Thank you," "You were

right, and I was wrong," or "Could you teach me about other things in life?" Instead, this is how Peter responded:

> When Simon Peter saw this, he fell at Jesus' knees and said, "Go away from me, Lord; I am a sinful man!" (Luke 5:8)

Peter's first response to being in the presence of Jesus, seeing Jesus' potential, and understanding the possibilities of what Jesus could do in one's life was, "Go away. You're so good, and I'm so bad. Someone like you shouldn't be anywhere near someone like me!" Jesus replied:

> Don't be afraid; from now on you will fish for people. (Luke 5:10)

I love that. In other words, Jesus said, "Listen here, Peter. I know you're afraid of me because you know that I'm good and you've made a ton of mistakes. You're afraid of me because you know enough about God and religion to understand how the whole sin and punishment thing works, and you think I'm going to give you what you deserve. If that were true and I were you, I'd be afraid of someone like me too.

"But how about this? How about from this point on,

your life becomes more than that of an ordinary fisher-man? Instead of sitting in this boat all day, how about you come and follow me? Let me show you a bigger, better purpose for your life."

Jesus didn't send Peter away. Instead, he called Peter to something bigger and better. From that point on, Peter followed Jesus, and Jesus began the process of un-dragoning Peter. Peter had given up on Jesus, but Jesus hadn't given up on Peter.

Fast-forward a few weeks in Peter's life. Peter had been following Jesus and learning from his teachings since that day in the boat. He had heard Jesus preach. He had seen Jesus perform amazing miracles. He had seen how Jesus took care of hungry people, dealt with criticism from cynics, and loved everyone he came in contact with. One day, after a particularly hard teaching, many of the people in the audience whom Jesus had offended began to grumble against him and his teachings. In fact, after Jesus was finished teaching, he lost many followers:

From this time many of his disciples turned back and no longer followed him. (John 6:66)

Imagine a modern-day preacher teaching actual, legitimate truth from the Bible and then immediately watching half his congregation get up and walk out the door never to return. That is exactly what happened after Jesus taught some hard but necessary truth. One moment, he was teaching to a big crowd. The next, it was just Jesus and his twelve friends standing in an open, empty field. Jesus then asked his friends a question:

> "You do not want to leave too, do you?" Jesus asked the Twelve. (John 6:67)

In other words, "Hey, guys. This is what you signed up for. I was serious about running after God's grace and truth. It's only going to get messier and more dangerous, and most people won't like what I have to say. So are you in? Or do you want to leave me too?"

I love Peter's response:

> Simon Peter answered him, "Lord, to whom shall we go? You have the words of eternal life. We have come to believe and to know that you are the Holy One of God." (John 6:68–69)

Peter responded, "Where else are we going to go? We are looking for truth, life, and a better path. We are looking for the one person in the universe who has the power to change what needs to be changed and heal what needs to be healed, and that person is you. Where else could we go to find that? Only you have the potential to make us better people. You're the only one who can save me, so I'm sticking with you. I'm not going anywhere."

In only a few short weeks, Peter had gone from believing he was a hopeless case to being one of Jesus' most loyal followers.

Why? Because Jesus gave Simon Peter a chance. Jesus didn't wait until Peter was a devout follower. While Peter was still a dragon, Jesus asked to be friends.

WHERE ELSE CAN DRAGONS GO?

Peter asked the ten-gazillion-dollar question: "Where else can dragons go in order to hear truth, find hope, and experience healing?" Only Jesus has the power to truly change anyone's life, so where is the most effective place for people to bump into Jesus if not the church?

To make this challenge hit closer to home, where else are Richard, Tony, and Jessica going to go, if not your church?

If dragons like Richard are ever going to be delivered from their struggles with sexual temptation, then they need a safe place in which Jesus can do all of the delivering.

And what about dragons like Tony? Tony had already been forgiven by God through Jesus, but Tony was struggling with forgiving himself. Tony saw Jesus and couldn't help but yell, "Go away from me, Jesus! I'm a sinful man." Tony was a new creation, but if he was ever going to view himself as more than a drug-addicted, racist convict, he was going to need to stand in the presence of Jesus and find a place where he could continually be reminded that God didn't hate him.

Or how about dragons like Jessica? I don't have any qualifications that allow me to sit down with Jessica and say, "Here's your problem, here's what you need to do to fix it, and if you follow these simple steps, everything will get better." That conversation will never take place. Only Jesus can possibly understand the dark, confusing places that led Jessica to make the decisions she made. I don't know if anything will ever change in the way that Jessica views herself and her gender, but I do know that if anything is ever going to change in her life, it will be because Jesus healed her.

Where else are dragons like Richard, Tony, and Jessica going to bump into Jesus, if not your church?

These are dragons' stories. These are the stories of people who, for various and complicated reasons, became people they were never intended to become. And if you think that their stories are more sinful than yours, or that Jesus' redeeming power is displayed more in their lives than in yours, then you need to take a long, hard look in the mirror. We are no different, and if we are ever going to have a shot at being rescued from our dragons, we need to be able to find and create communities where the saving mercy and grace of Jesus are on constant display.

At my doctor's appointment, at least my doctor was honest. Essentially, she said, "At my church, dragons are not safe. At my church, dragons aren't set free. We turn them away."

Are you too comfortable? Is your church content with being an unsafe environment for dragons? Or are you willing to take up the challenge of revitalizing your church into the hospital for dragons that Jesus originally intended?

If you're not willing to take up the challenge, then where else can dragons find a home?

9

SCARRED GUYS, SICK GUYS, AND SMALL STEPS

Do You Want to Be Whole?

In 2011, I had the opportunity to travel to the world's newest country at the time, South Sudan, in the middle of the African continent. Since that time, I have been traveling with teams back to this remote area at least twice a year in order to train and empower local pastors who are leading their villages and communities in the teaching of the gospel. We also assist in the creation and development of sustainable schools and medical clinics, and we microfinance for startup businesses.

The village in South Sudan that Flatirons is currently engaged with is called Maper, and it lies on the edge of the largest swamp in the world. The people of Maper are from the Dinka tribe, and they are some of the most beautiful people I have ever had the privilege of meeting. Their skin is the blackest of any race or tribe I've ever encountered, and they are incredibly tall. It is not unusual to look out over a gathering and see people who are more than seven feet tall. They are also thin. Very, very thin. Think Manute Bol, who played in the NBA in the 1980s and '90s. He was from Sudan, and he clocked in at seven feet and seven inches tall. (You should Google him right now if you don't know who I'm talking about.)

Other than their color, size, and height, the most noticeable characteristic of the Dinka people is their dignity. They are a people who live in one of the harshest environments in the world and have suffered through hundreds of years of genocidal tribal wars, but they still hold their heads high as they raise their crops, herd their cattle, and love and protect their families. They are amazing people.

During the rainy season, the Sudanese air is thick with mosquitos and other terrible insects. During the dry season, the temperature hovers around 120 degrees, and you can hardly see because the air is filled with dust and smoke. In the oppressive heat of the afternoon, life in Maper grinds to a halt, and everyone tries to find some shade in order to escape the equatorial sun and wait until life can continue in the early evening when the temperature cools to a crisp 80 to 90 degrees.

In Maper, there is a large tree where many of the village's men gather to discuss the latest political news, weather predictions, and the health of their cattle. On this first trip, as I sat with the other men under the tree, one of the Dinka tribesmen noticed the tattoo on my upper arm peeking out from under my short-sleeved shirt. He motioned toward my arm, asking me to pull up my sleeve so he could see the entire tattoo.

I lifted my sleeve. The tattoo covers my entire upper arm, and it is a picture of a dragon being torn to shreds by a giant lion. The tattoo is, of course, a symbol of the story that God used to un-dragon my life.

Before long, all the men were gathered around my arm as if I were a painting or sculpture in an art gallery. They had never seen anything like it before. A few started rubbing my arm to see if it would come off. Our translator began laughing and said, "They recognize a lion and a crocodile. They want to know what this picture means."

So I began relaying, with the help of our translator, the C. S. Lewis story and how it applies to Jesus and the process of becoming set free. The men listened to the story with wrinkled brows, occasionally muttering an, "Aay," whenever a particular part of the story resonated in their lives.

At the end, the men began talking among themselves, and our translator said, "They say it is a very good story."

Now it was my turn. One of the first things you will notice about the Dinka men, besides their towering height, is a series of horizontal scars that mark their foreheads from ear to ear. So I asked if they could help me understand the story of their scars. Over the next few minutes, they explained one of their most interesting rituals.

In the Dinka tribe, when a boy reaches the age of thirteen, he goes through a rite of passage that symbolizes his transformation from boyhood to manhood. The final ritual he must endure is a cutting ceremony where he sits in a chair while a village elder takes a razor-sharp blade and cuts through the skin, sometimes down to the bone, horizontally across the boy's forehead. Dug in the ground, directly under the boy, is a small hole to catch the flow of blood.

If the boy flinches or cries, he fails the test, and he is considered unfit to become a future husband and father. His family gathers behind the boy for support during the ceremony, but they also carry sticks and clubs to beat him if he fails the test. (How's that for motivation?) In the eyes of the Dinka people, if a boy can be trusted to endure this extremely painful ritual without flinching, crying, or running away, then you can count on him not to flinch, cry, or run away when life gets hard. He can be trusted to stand his ground, face the pain, and protect his family and village.

When they were done telling me the story of their scars, I said, "That is a very good story."

The men then asked me a question I was completely unprepared for: "In America, how does a boy become a man?"

I had no answer. I wanted to say, "We don't have any rites of passage for manhood in our culture anymore, which is why our country is filled with thirty-five-year-old little boys who still play video games and live in their parents' basements," but I didn't. The Dinka men's question stuck with me, and it still haunts me today.

I tell this story because I'm worried that many men and women in our world are too scared to take on their shares of responsibility in becoming men and women of God. I'm afraid that we're flinching. We make excuses. We run from anything we claim to be too hard or too painful.

Like the Dinka tribe's ritual, there has to come a moment in our lives when we snap out of it and decide to become the men and women we were created to be, rather than remain twenty-, thirty-, forty-, or eighty-year-old little boys and girls.

We need to have clear markers of those moments of transformation. The process will require a lot of courage, and it will cause a lot of pain. The process will leave us scarred. But we must realize that, while Jesus is the only one who slays dragons, there are responsibilities we need to carry and steps we need to take to participate in the slaying. At some point, theorizing about being free isn't enough. Eventually we need to sit down in that chair, bear through the pain, and undergo the ritual of facing our own dragons.

Jesus wants to rip away the dragon scales. He wants to point you toward the better life that you were created to enjoy. But you are responsible for taking a few steps in order for Jesus to begin the process of setting you free.

So what are those steps?

DO YOU WANT TO BE WHOLE?

One day, as Jesus was walking through Jerusalem, he came to a famous pool. The pool was famous because people believed its waters had magic powers. They believed an angel would periodically come down from heaven and stir the pool, and the first one into the bubbling waters would be healed.

Jesus walked toward the water's edge and noticed it was surrounded by a great number of disabled people who were trapped inside bodies that didn't work anymore.

One who was there had been an invalid for thirty-eight years. When Jesus saw him lying there and learned that he had been in this condition for a long time, he asked him, "Do you want to get well?"

"Sir," the invalid replied, "I have no one to help me into the pool when the water is stirred. While I am trying to get in, someone else goes down ahead of me."

Then Jesus said to him, "Get up! Pick up your mat and walk." At once the man was cured; he picked up his mat and walked. (John 5:5–9)

I think Jesus' question was peculiar. He approached a pool surrounded by people with all kinds of disabilities, walked up to a guy who had been sick for thirty-eight years, and asked him a no-brainer: "Do you want to get well?"

If you were that sick guy, how do you think you would have answered Jesus' question? I know how I would have answered: "Let's see. For the past thirty-eight years, I have been trapped inside a body that isn't able to do what I need it to do. So for nearly four decades, I have been an invalid, and now you're asking if I want to get well?

"Yes! Yes, yes, yes. I've been sitting here for years. I'm sick of being sick. I've had enough, and nothing I've tried has ever worked. Apparently, I've been doing it wrong. Just tell me what to do. Yes, I want to get well!"

That's what I would have said had Jesus asked me the same question. However, that was not how the man replied. Read it again:

"Sir," the invalid replied, "I have no one to help me into the pool when the water is stirred. While I am trying to get in, someone else goes down ahead of me." (John 5:7)

In other words, "I can't get well. No one will help me. I've tried before, and it doesn't work. Something always goes wrong. Somebody cuts me off, takes my turn, or gets there before I do."

Remember the donkey Eeyore from *Winnie the Pooh*? Listen to the Eeyore in this guy's answer: "Poor me. Nobody cares about me. Nobody helps me. It's not my fault. I want to get well, but it probably won't work. You all can go ahead. I'll just sit here for another thirty-eight years."

We all have Eeyores in our lives. When you mention that it's a nice day, they reply, "Probably gonna rain." When you ask how they're doing, they reply, "Bad. Divorced. Alone. Depressed. Abandoned. Unemployed. Overweight. In debt. Angry. Bitter."

I don't mean to minimize the pain, trauma, and horror of all those situations. Robin and I know the hell of walking through years of sickness and depression. However, there is a problem when we allow the circumstances of our lives, especially the hard ones, to define us.

Jesus doesn't want us to be defined by our circumstances.

He wants to take our experiences, good and bad, and use them to mold us into the people he originally intended.

Let's take a closer look at the words of Jesus when he asked, "Do you want to get well?" (John 5:6). The word "well" in that question is the Greek word *hugios*. This word literally translates as "whole." So Jesus asked the man, "Do you want to be whole?"

I love that question. Do you want to be whole? Do want to experience the whole, better, abundant life that God created for you?

It inspires me to think Jesus did not choose the Greek word *sozo*, which translates as "saved" or "healed." Most of the time, when Jesus performed a miracle, especially one that healed someone from sickness or physical disability, the miracle was a picture of the eternal healing of our souls from the sickness of sin and separation from God. When Jesus performed those miracles, he frequently used the word *sozo* to talk about the saving and healing that was available to people through Jesus.

However, in this story about the man at the pool of Bethesda, Jesus used the word *hugios* for "whole" instead of the word *sozo* for "saved" or "healed." Why?

I don't think Jesus was talking about spiritual or eternal salvation with the sick man at the pool. I believe he was talking about the quality of life that was available to the man in the here and now. Let the differences between the two sink in because this is going to hit close to home for many of you.

I think Jesus was teaching that it is possible to believe all of the right stuff, have your sins taken away through Jesus' death and resurrection, have a guaranteed spot in heaven, have the Holy Spirit take up shop in your life, and *still* waste the life on earth that God has given you.

Many of us have subscribed to the idea that Jesus' grace, mercy, forgiveness, and holiness are sufficient enough to cleanse us from sin and get us out of hell, but they aren't sufficient enough to address the pain and injustice that have attacked our lives in the here and now. Many of us know that if we were to drop dead while reading this book, we would go to heaven; yet while we have assurance of eternal salvation, we also have a sense that we've been abandoned and isolated in our current lives.

Many of us have had the following conversation with God: "Thank you, God, for saving me on an eternal, spiritual level. But I have no one to help me out here on earth. Nothing will ever change, and what's worse, none of this is my fault."

Jesus says, "I didn't ask whose fault this was. I didn't ask how you got to this point in your life. The bigger, better question I'm asking is, 'Do you want to be *whole*?'"

To that question, many of us respond, "Jesus, my life is probably out of your league. My story is different. You know the ways in which I've been hurt. You know about the sickness in my marriage, my divorce, and my family. You shouldn't be asking if I want to be whole because you should know that it's impossible."

The truth, however, is that Jesus' grace *is* sufficient. In Jesus, you *can* have peace, and you *can* overcome being a victim of your current circumstances.

The question is not, "Do you know *how* to become whole?"

Thankfully, the question is simply, "Do you *want* to be whole?"

It's up to you to answer that question. If you've decided you want to be whole, then there are some small steps you need to begin taking. These steps may sound insignificant, but if you skip them, nothing will ever change in your life. Jesus can't take these steps for you. He can help you with them, but you are the one who must choose to face your dragons.

I am in no way presenting "three easy steps to wholeness." When it comes to the darkest corners of our lives, there are no three easy steps for anything. But I have discovered that we're not going to move an inch toward a life of wholeness unless our journey includes these three steps. They are nonnegotiable, not optional, and absolutely vital. The three steps are to change your mind, stop making excuses, and do what needs to be done.

CHANGE YOUR MIND

Let's start with the first step. The Bible has a specific word for the idea of changing your mind. The word is *repentance*: "God, I've had enough. This is not the life I want. I want the life you intended for me."

I once attended a seminar called Financial Peace, led by Dave Ramsey. Financial Peace is an excellent course on money management, and it's especially useful to those of us who have continued to abuse loans and credit cards until we find ourselves drowning in debt. One thing in particular stood out to me from this course, and it was Ramsey's definition of *insanity* that I believe he borrowed from someone else: "Insanity is doing the same thing over and over, but expecting a different result each time."[1]

Ramsey applied this definition of insanity to debt and foolish spending, but it fits perfectly for many areas of life, especially the dark ones. Insanity is continuing to make poor decisions and partake in bad habits while simultaneously expecting our lives to get better. It's utter insanity, and if we ever want to change, then we need to start by breaking that cycle. We need to wake up and say, "Enough! No more. This is not the life for me. I don't want more of the same. It's time for something new and something better."

This is called repentance. This is changing your mind.

You might ask, "But what about all my bitterness? What about all my guilt? Those aren't easy to erase."

You could probably build an argument for why you deserve to be bitter and angry about your current circumstances, and I'll bet that most people would agree with you. They might even say, "If I were you, I'd be bitter too." The problem is that this bitterness is ruining everything else in your life. It's probably safe to say that you're now bitter about much more than the initial circumstances that sparked your anger. The bitterness has spread like a disease to every area of your life.

As far as the guilt goes, guilt is a natural response to sin. We feel guilty because we *are* guilty. We've disobeyed God. However, guilt is only meant to get our attention so that we realize we need to change our minds. Guilt is supposed to be a tool that enables us to leave behind our current, destructive patterns and choose God's better way.

While guilt is a useful tool, Jesus came to remove it so that we don't have to carry it around for the rest of our lives. God has already forgiven us; now we need to work on forgiving ourselves and unloading the guilt.

Do you want to be whole? Then you need to repent. You need to change your mind. You need to have a heart-to-heart with God: *Dear God, I don't want to be stuck in this cycle of insanity. I don't want just a portion of life. I want the whole thing. I've changed my mind about settling for a lesser life. I now want a whole, abundant life. Please forgive me for settling for less than your best for me. Make me whole. In Jesus' name, amen.*

STOP MAKING EXCUSES

When you change your mind, your next step is to stop making excuses.

If you've truly changed your mind, then you should be trying to see your situation differently. You're no longer going to lie by the side of the pool while life goes on without you. In the story about the sick guy by the pool, it didn't matter *how* he got there or *why* he'd been stuck there for thirty-eight years. Maybe no one would help him into the pool. Maybe people cut him off before he had the chance to be cured. Regardless of how he got there, it wasn't helping the man's cause to sit around and point out the injustice of his situation.

It doesn't help anyone to sit around and make excuses.

This is directly applicable to our lives. The person who abused you shouldn't have. Your spouse shouldn't have dishonored his or her promise to you and God. Your mother or father shouldn't have abandoned you. It's not fair that you're sick, single, broke, fat, or skinny. For many of us, the incident that set us on the wrong tracks wasn't even our fault.

Regardless of your circumstances, beginning the process of becoming whole is entirely up to you. The Holy Spirit is prodding you. He's tapping you on the shoulder and whispering in your ear, but you have to decide whether or not you're going to listen. You are the one who needs to change your mind. You are the one who needs to stop making excuses.

If you decide to change your mind and quit making excuses, Jesus won't look at you and say, "Good. Then it's up to you to figure it out all by yourself. You need to find strength inside yourself. If you stick out your chin, pull yourself up by your bootstraps, try harder, and think positive thoughts, then everything will work out."

No. Jesus is saying that you alone are responsible for taking the small steps toward changing your mind and ceasing your excuses, but after that, he will give you the sufficient strength and direction in order to shed your scales. He will never tell you to find the strength and direction on your own because that's impossible. You don't have the strength necessary to fix your life. If you did, you would have changed by now.

God will never give you a command without also providing whatever you need to carry that command out. Paul said it this way:

I can do all this through him who gives me strength. (Philippians 4:13)

Notice that Paul didn't say, "I can do all this if I try harder, never give up, and find the strength within myself." Instead, Paul said that whatever circumstances he would face, whether good or bad, he would prevail because, through Christ, nothing is impossible. Paul recognized that, on his own, he didn't stand a chance. But he also recognized that he wasn't on his own. He knew he had Christ living inside him, and because of that, he could accomplish whatever God asked him to accomplish.

God's promise to offer strength and direction must have been crucial to the foundation of Paul's life, because he returned to that theme over and over. Here is another description from Paul of God's promises to us:

We know that in all things God works for the good of those who love him, who have been called according to his purpose. For those God foreknew he also predestined to be conformed to the likeness of his Son, that he might be the firstborn among many brothers. And those he predestined, he also called; those he called, he also justified; those he justified, he also glorified.

What, then, shall we say in response to this? If God is for us, who can be against us? He who did not spare his own Son, but gave him up for us all—how will he not also, along with him, graciously give us all things? Who will bring any charge against those whom

God has chosen? It is God who justifies. Who is he that condemns? Christ Jesus, who died—more than that, who was raised to life—is at the right hand of God and is also interceding for us. Who shall separate us from the love of Christ? Shall trouble or hardship or persecution or famine or nakedness or danger or sword? As it is written:

> *"For your sake we face death all day long;*
> *we are considered as sheep to be slaughtered."*

No, in all these things we are more than conquerors through him who loved us. For I am convinced that neither death nor life, neither angels nor demons, neither the present nor the future, nor any powers, neither height nor depth, nor anything else in all creation, will be able to separate us from the love of God that is in Christ Jesus our Lord. (Romans 8:28–39)

God promises to use all things for our benefit. This includes our good circumstances as well as our troubled, dark circumstances. This includes the parts of our lives that we screwed up with our bad decisions and habits. This includes the parts of our lives that were screwed up by someone else who hurt us and robbed us. Whatever it is that left us lying by the pool, broken, hurting, and damaged for years—whatever it is that dragoned us—God says that he can use everything, bright or dark, to create something good in our lives.

We need to change our minds about continuing to live locked up in the belly of the dragon. We need to quit making excuses. What happened, happened. We cannot change it. It would be awesome if we could undo our pasts, but that isn't an option. We need to allow God to take that past and turn it into something good.

DO WHAT NEEDS TO BE DONE

The third step, after you change your mind and quit making excuses, is to do what needs to be done. In chapter 6, I used this application as one example of the many ways we can carry the burdens of hurting people. But this step also applies to ourselves when *we* are the hurting people.

I believe the majority of you reading this book are now experiencing an annoying voice in your head that says, *You know exactly what he's talking about. You know exactly what needs to be done.*

Sometimes that voice is a quiet whisper. Other times it feels like a two-by-four smacking you upside the head. That voice, big or small, is called the Holy Spirit. He is in the line of work called *conviction*. His specialty is taking the truth of God's Word and bringing it to life within you.

The question you need to wrestle with right now is not, "What does Jim think I should do?" The question is, "What is the Holy Spirit telling me to do?" You probably don't even need to pray for God to reveal it to you; you already know. You probably don't need to figure out what needs to be done; you only need to decide whether or not you're going to do it. Do you *want* to be whole?

In case you're one of the very few who don't know what you're supposed to do, I'll throw out one specific. At Flatirons, one of our six core values is called "Gifted Service." Gifted Service is based on the biblical truth that every Christian has the presence of Christ living inside him or her, and when Christ takes up residence in a person, he brings with him spiritual gifts that allow that person to participate in the mission to bring Christ to a lost and broken world. Furthermore, every Christian has some combination of the fruit of the Spirit, which allows a person to better reflect the personality and attitude of Jesus to everyone he or she comes in contact with.

The church is described as the body of Christ (Romans 12; 1 Corinthians 12). This means that if the church is going to be healthy, function at its full redemptive potential, and have a maximum impact on our communities and our world, then we are going to need every person— every arm, every leg, every finger, every nose—working, serving, praying, giving, and partnering in the revolutionary mission that God has called us to join. No individual can be just like Christ, but together as the church, we can carry out the ministry of reconciliation and redemption that Jesus has commissioned us to carry out.

Very few people have a problem with that biblical truth. However, many pew potatoes get upset with the logical conclusion that follows that truth: if you are a Christian who has put your entire hope and faith in Jesus as your Lord, Master, Controller, and Savior; and if you've been attending your church for a while but have no plans to serve, give, partner with, or invite others to your church and all you ever do is show up on the weekend, criticize the teachings that don't align with your personal preferences, and slip out early; then you aren't contributing anything to the mission of Christ. I encourage you to find another church where you *can* serve, you *can* give, and you *can* partner with others because, if you stay at your current church, you are only going to infect the body of Christ with the disease of cynicism.

If you've changed your mind and quit making excuses, but you don't know what needs to be done next, then I encourage you to partner with a church that you trust in order to join in the mission of redemption that God wants to spread throughout the world.

I want to clarify that this truth is only for those of

you who have begun the process of healing. There are times and seasons of your life when the sufficient strength that Christ provides will only be the strength enough to make it through another day, and that's okay. Take all of the time you need. The church is a safe place to heal. In Ecclesiastes, Solomon wrote:

> *[There is] a time to weep and a time to laugh,*
> *a time to mourn and a time to dance.* (Ecclesiastes 3:4)

You will have seasons of weeping, mourning, sadness, and pain, but they are seasons, not lifetimes. Eventually you will find that he has given you the strength to make it through the week. Then you'll discover he has given you the strength to make it through the month, and then the year. God has the ability to heal you.

> *You turned my wailing into dancing;*
> *you removed my sackcloth and clothed me with joy.*
> (Psalm 30:11)

If you were to break your arm today, the doctor would wrap it in a cast, put it in a sling, and tell you not to use it for a little while. Sometimes we simply need to sit and heal. However, if I were to ask you why you weren't using your arm, and you were to respond, "I broke it three years ago," then your issue is much more than just a broken arm, right?

Therefore, if you've changed your mind and quit making excuses, then do what needs to be done. If your broken bones have healed enough to be used again, then listen to that nagging voice in your head and do what it is telling you. Maybe that voice is telling you to make a long overdue phone call to a counselor, a pastor, a doctor, a lawyer, the police, or an old friend. Maybe that voice is telling you to forgive one of your enemies. Maybe it is telling you to forgive your spouse, your ex, or your parents. Whatever the Holy Spirit is telling you to do, go and do it. Take that step.

If you've healed enough to get to work, but you aren't clear about what the Holy Spirit is saying, then jump into a church community you trust. Begin praying with that community. Begin inviting your friends. Begin offering your time, talents, and treasures to the mission of Christ.

Jesus asked if you want to be whole. So now, I'm asking you. Do you want to be whole? Or do you want to stay a dragon?

Do you want the whole and abundant life that Jesus offers? Do you want to become a man or woman of God? Or have you surrendered to the idea that your life will only ever be a fraction of the one intended for you? Are you too scared to undergo the ritual of facing your dragons? Jesus is the one who un-dragons, but you have some steps you need to take if you want him to begin that process. You have a choice.

If you desire your life, your family's lives, or the life of your church to be freed from the dragon, then you must take ownership of your responsibility in that un-dragoning. If you want to be whole, then you must undergo the painful but powerful process of allowing God to tear away the scales. Like those Dinka boys, you place a marker that will forever state, "That was the moment I became something different. That was the moment I took on responsibility for my life. That was when I changed my mind, quit making excuses, and began doing what needed to be done. That was the moment I endured the ritual of facing my dragons."

10

TRUTH, GRACE, AND
SPIRITUAL POVERTY

Being Un-Dragoned Is Better, Not Always Easier

I wish I could end this book at chapter 9 without having a guilty conscience. I wish I could have shared my story; walked through the different ways God tears the scales from our families, friends, and churches; offered a few ideas for initial steps toward a life with no more dragons; and then ended with a simple, encouraging, fluff-piece outro.

But I've never been a fan of ignoring the difficult parts of life, so I won't start now.

Here's the truth: allowing God to tear the scales from your life is better. I would never deny that a life without dragons is better. Yet I would be lying if I didn't warn you that an un-dragoned life is often a more difficult life.

Being un-dragoned is better, not always easier.

Jesus frees us from our dragons by perfectly sharing both grace and truth in our lives. Therefore, as freed people, we are supposed to mimic Jesus by consistently displaying both grace and truth to our lost and broken world. We must hold to grace as fiercely as we hold to truth, and the two foundations must exist in equal parts if we don't want our lives to crumble. Unfortunately I have discovered that too many people prefer one or the other. They either want to hold to truth and ignore grace, or vice versa.

Here is the warning I need to share with you: if you attempt to equally hold to grace and truth, just as Jesus displayed in his own life here on earth, then you are going to be shot at from both sides. The people who favor grace will say you're hateful, and the people who favor truth will say you've watered down the Bible. If you hold to grace and truth in the same way that Jesus did, you will find a whole slew of brand-new enemies. After all, Jesus was crucified for the way he lived.

So how do we prepare ourselves for the difficult job of holding equally to both grace *and* truth?

CONTROVERSIAL BEATITUDES

The Sermon on the Mount was Jesus' first public talk to receive a full manuscript in the gospels, and this manuscript opens with a section that has been labeled "The Beatitudes." We don't use the word *beatitude* in modern language, but the concept should sound familiar. A beatitude is a wise saying or proverb. For example, "The early bird gets the worm," "All work and no play makes Jack a dull boy," or "A rolling stone gathers no moss," could all be considered beatitudes. They are little sayings that sound simple but hold deeper truth and instruction.

Beatitudes are still important to Middle Eastern culture today. The first time I visited Afghanistan, I was invited to address a group of Afghan men. Just before the event, our host moved us indoors due to security. When I asked what the threat was, he replied, "Grenades." I should have known right away that this speaking engagement was going to be much different than the kind I was used to in the States.

Our host asked me to begin my talk with a parable or a wise saying. I had no idea what he meant, so he gave me an example of a popular Afghan beatitude: "The first time we meet, we are strangers. The second time, we are friends. The third time, we are brothers."

My mind went blank. I couldn't think of a single wise saying from American culture. In fact, the only sayings that came to my mind all rhymed with Nantucket, so those wouldn't work. Eventually I thought of one. I ran it by our host, and to my great surprise, he loved it. So I stood up in front of four hundred Afghan men, some of whom were still Taliban, and I loudly proclaimed, "Blessed is the man who has a big wife. She keeps him warm in the winter and gives him shade in the summer."

A brief moment of silence followed that felt like an eternity, and all I could think about was my host's nonchalant warning about grenades. But to my relief, the room soon fell to pieces in laughter and cheering. In most of the world, larger women are signs of wealth. They mean that their husbands have enough money to buy their families food. So the Afghan men loved my beatitude. The two American women from my team were another story. They glared at me from across the room, but the crowd was filled with members of the Taliban, so they couldn't say anything. (Trust me, I received an earful when we were back in a safer environment.)

Anyway, those are examples of beatitudes, and just for the record, Jesus' beatitudes are much better than mine. They're not less controversial, but they're better.

Let's jump back to Jesus' first documented sermon. Jesus was starting to draw some large crowds. Unfortunately, he wasn't drawing crowds because of what he was teaching. He was drawing crowds of people who wanted to watch him perform miracles like some kind of ancient magic show. So whenever Jesus taught a group, it was usually comprised of several different types of people.

Some of the people in the crowd had no interest in God, Jesus, or anyone else telling them what to do or how to live their lives. They were simply looking for someone to quickly fix their problems or remove their obstacles so that they could continue living their lives as they had before.

When they prayed, it sounded like this: *Dear God, heal my body, fix my kid, and send more money so I can get on with the plans I have for my life. Thanks. I'll look you up when I have another problem. See you later.*

Another group in the crowd was made up of religious people. They took it upon themselves to build a list of sins and grade them on a scale of "worst sin ever" to "that barely counts as a sin." To no one's surprise, the sins that they personally struggled with were always on the "that barely counts as a sin" end of the spectrum. These religious people decided it was their duty to use God's Word to hunt down, punish, threaten, and beat up people who erred on the "worst sin ever" side of the spectrum.

When they prayed, it sounded like this: *Dear God, I'm thankful that I'm not as bad as those other people. I know you don't love them, so I'll help out and beat them up for you. You're welcome. In your name, amen.*

The other group in the crowd was made up of people who had turned away from God's grace and truth. Some of them had been treated poorly by the religious crowd. They believed the lie that God hated them, and after carrying all that guilt, shame, and condemnation for so long, they eventually decided to avoid the subject of God entirely. Others had, on their own accord, simply let go of the concepts of biblical truth, God's grace, and the reality of sin. They ignored the verses of the Bible that didn't subscribe to their political views, and they shopped around until finding a belief system that fell in line with their own desires.

If they prayed at all, it sounded like this: *Dear God, Goddess, Spiritual Energy Love Force of the Universe that exists in us all . . . I'm going to do what I think is right in my own eyes, and nobody has the right to tell me what to do. In my own name, amen.*

If you're anything like me, you're chuckling right now because you realize that the world and culture that Jesus walked around in wasn't very different from the world and culture we find ourselves in today. In fact, when I teach on the weekends, I guarantee you that one person from each of those groups is in attendance at every service.

So Jesus stood in front of a large crowd that looked incredibly similar to the ones you'd find in most churches today, and five minutes into his opening remarks, he made the following statement:

> Blessed are you when people insult you, persecute you and falsely say all kinds of evil against you because of me. Rejoice and be glad, because great is your reward in heaven, for in the same way they persecuted the prophets who were before you. (Matthew 5:11–12)

Essentially, Jesus claimed that if you decide to believe in and embrace his definition of a better way to experience a full life, then there will be groups of people who will line up to hate you, attack you, and say evil things against you. Jesus reminded the people that it had already been done to the prophets before them, and there would be more of the same in the future.

The majority of the crowd were likely confused by Jesus' words, but I wouldn't be surprised if Jesus jumped a few months ahead in his mind. He was thinking about what was going to happen to him on a cross. He knew he wasn't going to be crucified for teaching things like, "Can't we all just get along and mind our own business?" He knew he was going to be crucified for saying things like:

> I am the way and the truth and the life. No one comes to the Father except through me. (John 14:6)

When you think about it, of all the statements that Jesus ever made, that would be one of the most offensive, divisive, and arrogant—*if* it were untrue. But if true, it's one of the most loving statements he ever made.

Jesus also said controversial things like:

If you hold to my teaching, you are really my disciples. Then you will know the truth, and the truth will set you free. (John 8:31–32)

In fact, after Jesus made that comment, an argument began ringing from the crowd who claimed they were already free without Jesus telling them what to do. They picked up rocks and tried to shut Jesus up by stoning him to death.

Jesus wasn't crucified for being one of those "everything is cool, let's just get along" hippies. He was crucified because he made controversial statements about being the Son of God. And in his first documented public teaching, Jesus warned his followers, "If you decide to follow me and genuinely hold onto my truth and grace, then I can promise that you will accumulate enemies. Some of them might even try to crucify you like they will do to me."

In short, Jesus made the following offer to his people: "I'm giving you one last chance to run for the door. But if you choose to stick with me, we're going to walk into a storm."

I now offer the same to you. If you want the application you pull from this book to be simple and easy, then quit reading now. Just put the book down. But if you want to hold equally to both Jesus' grace and truth, then you need to read on and prepare yourself for the storm.

SPIRITUAL POVERTY

At the beginning of Jesus' Sermon on the Mount, he claimed that the following was necessary in order for any person to enjoy a whole and abundant life:

> Now when he saw the crowds, he went up on a moun-
> tainside and sat down. His disciples came to him, and
> he began to teach them, saying:
> "Blessed are the poor in spirit, for theirs is the
> kingdom of heaven." (Matthew 5:1–3)

That statement doesn't immediately sound controversial, so let's break it down.

First of all, Jesus started out on a happy note: "Blessed are . . ." The first two words of his sermon sounded like Jesus brought everybody to the top of that hill to announce three simple, easy steps that would ensure happiness, financial security, and a long, healthy life. To be fair, that's what many of us think when we hear the word "blessed," right?

When we hear the word "blessed," we think, *The Lord blessed us with a beautiful baby. The Lord blessed my company, so we made a lot of money and bought a big house. The Lord has blessed my family, and that's why we're happy and healthy.*

I'm not sure that using the word "blessed" is always a bad thing, but in the context of Jesus' sermon, "blessed" is translated from the Greek word *makarios*, and it has nothing whatsoever to do with the happiness we so often connect to our circumstances, health, family, or savings account. Instead, *makarios* literally translates, "Full of God; fully and wholly satisfied in God; connected to God and having God live in you."[1]

At first, *makarios* sounds great. The word feels positive and affirming, and it makes us happy. But that's only until we read the rest of Jesus' statement, and we discover where true blessing is found:

> "Blessed are the poor in spirit, for theirs is the kingdom of heaven." (Matthew 5:3)

The word "poor" in this sentence literally translates, "To crouch or cower like a beggar in abject poverty and complete destitution; unable to help oneself; dependent on the alms or gifts of someone else."[2]

At first glance, that sounds like something Jesus would say: "I really love poor people." And Jesus does love poor people. But in this sermon, he was specifically talk-ing about the poverty and brokenness we find within our souls. He was talking about spiritual poverty.

The spirit that Jesus referred to is the part of you that makes you . . . well, *you*. It's not the flesh, blood, and bone. It's the spirit that God breathed into you that gives you life. It's the real, deep-down part of you. It's your identity, your soul.

After those opening remarks in Jesus' sermon, I'm sure some people were confused. The group who had expected healing tricks and positive life lessons probably leaned back on their elbows and squinted at Jesus with "what did you just say?" looks on their faces. And I don't blame them. Jesus made an odd statement. He said, "If any of you want to live in *makarios* with God and participate fully in the abundant life he has in mind for you, then you must come to the real-ization that you are hopeless. I'm not talking about your circumstances, body, or abilities. I'm talking about your soul. Your spirit is poor, empty, broken, and unable to heal itself."

To sum it up in one sentence, Jesus said, "Blessed are you when you realize that you have nothing to offer spiri-tually, because then, and only then, will you be ready to have me as king of your life."

There are two applications I want to pull from that statement. The first is internal. We have to realize that in order to begin Jesus' rule and dominion over our hearts, we must first come to God with a sense of spiritual poverty. We must admit that we are empty, broken, and incapable of fixing ourselves, and we must become beggars at the feet of Jesus. We must ask to be filled with God's Spirit, and we have to let go of our own selfish conditions, desires, and expectations for what we think God's command over our lives should look like.

The second application is more external. The teaching that Jesus offered to his followers two thousand years ago still holds true for his church today. If we, as a church, are going to effectively bring Jesus' kingdom to a lost, fallen, and broken world, then the church needs to become beggars who collectively admit we are only satisfied through Jesus. As a church, our only credential should read, "We were hopeless and alone, but Jesus saved us and continues to save us."

Whether we've attended church for sixty years or we walked through the front doors for the first time last weekend, we must never lose the culture of spiritual poverty that Jesus claims will bring about his kingdom of heaven in this world. We can never view ourselves as having figured it all out. The church shouldn't appear as a bunch of perfect people who are telling a bunch of jacked-up people how to quit being evil. The church should be comprised of nothing more than beggars showing other beggars where to find food.

DOES BEING TRUTHFUL EQUAL BEING JUDGMENTAL?

If I'm hanging over a cliff by a chain, and you're hanging on another chain right next to me, how many links of the chain do we have to break before we fall to our deaths? One. You only have to break one link, and it doesn't even matter which link it is. It doesn't matter if you only break one, while I break hundreds. In the end, we both have the same, equal problem. We've sinned and fallen.

Nobody who picks up this book is better or worse than anyone else. Personally, I have nothing to offer you. Pastor Jim is no better or worse than anyone else. Just because I wrote a book and lead a church doesn't mean I can save anybody. I certainly haven't done anything to save myself. I can't change, fix, or convert anybody, and I'm also not in charge of what God decides to be sin or free game. Even if I wanted to (and I certainly don't), I am not capable of changing God's definition of truth.

The only thing I can do is point toward Jesus. The only teaching I'm allowed to offer is the truth I find in Jesus' description for a better life. You don't have to like it. You don't have to agree with it. You don't have to line up your life with it. But none of that changes the fact that God declared certain ways of life sinful, and other ways life-giving.

Some people think I'm being judgmental because I

stand by God's description of an abundant life: "Jim, you sound judgmental. It sounds like you think that if I ignore what God says is best and true, then that makes me wrong."

News flash: it does. And thankfully, it's not because I said so, but only because Jesus said so.

I've often heard the following from people I meet on the weekends: "Jesus didn't come to judge people, Jim. So you don't have the right to tell me what I should do with my life. You're taking what Jesus said out of context, and you're using it to push your own opinions on other people."

I want to address that common view. Most people don't realize that whenever you see Jesus saying, "I didn't come to judge the world, but to save the world," he is making that statement because everyone is *already* under judgment. That's simply how it works. God spoke truth, and we've all fallen short of it because we are all equal in our spiritual poverty. Jesus doesn't need to judge anyone, because we've already been condemned.

Jesus came to save us from the condemnation that naturally follows our sin. Whenever people who favor grace over truth use the whole "Jesus didn't come to judge anyone" verse as ammunition, I always ask them to read the rest of that passage:

> As for the person who hears my words but does not keep them, I do not judge him. For I did not come to judge

the world, but to save it. There is a judge for the one who rejects me and does not accept my words; that very word which I spoke will condemn him at the last day. For I did not speak of my own accord, but the Father who sent me commanded me what to say and how to say it. I know that his command leads to eternal life. So whatever I say is just what the Father has told me to say. (John 12:47–50)

Essentially Jesus said, "I came to save you from the consequences of rejecting what God says leads to eternal life. I came to save you from the condemnation that comes from ignoring what God said was truth and sin. I'm not judging you. I'm saving you. But heads-up: there *is* a judge."

In that statement, Jesus perfectly displayed equal amounts of truth and grace.

Another practical example of Jesus' truth and grace occurs during the story about the woman caught in adultery that I recounted in chapter 2. When the religious men threw the naked woman at Jesus' feet, they quoted the biblical law that declared stoning as the punishment for adultery. The interesting part of this story that many people either ignore or miss is that Jesus agreed with the religious people. He said, "You're right. The wages of sin is death" (paraphrased from Romans 6:23).

Jesus didn't ignore the truth of the situation. However, he followed it with grace. He said, "If any of you are perfect, go ahead and toss the first stone. If any of you are quali-fied, you can kick off this good, old-fashioned stoning." Of course, the crowd wasn't qualified, so they left. Jesus, who was the only qualified person in the crowd, didn't so much as touch a rock:

> Jesus straightened up and asked her, "Woman, where are they? Has no one condemned you?"
>
> "No one, sir," she said.
>
> "Then neither do I condemn you," Jesus declared. "Go now and leave your life of sin." (John 8:10–11)

Here is the aspect of Jesus' grace that we can't miss. Jesus didn't refuse to condemn the woman because he thought adultery was okay or didn't matter. The Word of God had already passed judgment on the wrongness of adultery. Instead of giving her what she deserved for her sin (and it was absolutely a sin), Jesus offered her a way out of her condemnation. Directly after leading with grace, Jesus offered truth:

> . . . and leave your life of sin. (John 8:11)

Jesus didn't say, "I don't condemn you. So get back to that hotel room, keep on doing whatever you think will make you happy, and don't let anyone tell you what is wrong or right for your life. My love and forgiveness are blank checks so that you can do whatever you want."

Jesus also didn't say, "The wages of sin is death," and then stone the poor girl.

Jesus said, "The life you're living is sinful. I want to forgive you for that because I offer grace. But I also offer truth, so you must leave your sin if you want an abundant life."

No, Jesus didn't come to judge us, but that's because we've already been judged. We've all broken links of the chain. We've all fallen.

A TARGET FOR BOTH SIDES

One of the things I love most about Flatirons Community Church is that we are a community that is distinctly and outspokenly trying to hold to both grace *and* truth, instead of grace *or* truth.

Truth without grace results in hammering people over the head with what God says to be true.

Grace without truth results in patting people on the head and telling them to do whatever they want because "all is forgiven."

Many Christians and churches choose one over the other, but at Flatirons, we're trying to hold to both. As a pastor, I'm trying to teach that what God says is true, admit that we've fallen short of it, and make clear that we all deserve condemnation for our sin. But I'm also trying to teach that because God loves us, we are forgiven through Jesus so that we can continue running after God. Because of Christ's sacrifice we are no longer condemned.

As I mentioned, the problem with hanging on to both grace and truth is that it makes you a target for both sides. When I preach grace, then the truth people, who pretend like they don't wrestle with any sin, say, "You're watering down the Word of God and being too easy on sinners." When I preach truth, then the grace people, who pretend like sin doesn't exist, say, "You're mean. You just don't understand. If you loved someone who was struggling with that particular issue, you'd feel differently."

Rather than try to biblically justify every single thing I say to every single person who doesn't like it, I usually lie low and don't push back.

One time, however, I decided to speak up—and it was a mistake.

It wasn't a mistake because of what I said. I still stand by the truth of what I said. But I screwed up because of where I said it: on my Facebook page. Social media websites are simply not the appropriate forums in which to discuss emotionally charged issues. Tone and intention are difficult to gather on Facebook, so my post was torn to shreds by both sides of the truth and grace argument.

Heck, I'm about to retell the story in this book, and I'm pretty sure there will be some readers who will immediately dismiss the other nine chapters simply because of one or two phrases that they will choose to read in isolation. I hope that you read the following without favoring one side over the other, whether it's grace or truth.

So what did I say on Facebook?

In early 2013, I was receiving many e-mails from friends who were asking for perspective on the gay-marriage debate that was front and center, not only in Colorado legislature but also in the Supreme Court. One of the recurring questions was, "What did Jesus say about gay marriage?"

That is a great question. A bad question would be, "Jim, what do *you* say about gay marriage?" or, "What is Flatirons's position on gay marriage?"

"What did Jesus say about gay marriage?" is a great question, and here's the answer: *nothing.* Nothing at all.

However, I knew that homosexuality was a tough, emotional, and potentially volatile subject for many people, especially those of us at Flatirons who were either gay or loved someone who was gay. So via Facebook, I decided to give what I thought was a simple, loving perspective on the social issue. I did what I always try to do. I always try to point at Jesus and say, "Here's what he said." In this case, Jesus didn't say much, so I searched Scripture for anything that Jesus had to say about marriage in general. In every case, he referred back to God joining one man and one woman together in spiritual, relational, and physical intimacy. Here's an example of one of those statements:

> "Haven't you read," he replied, "that at the beginning the Creator 'made them male and female,' and said, 'For this reason a man will leave his father and mother and be united to his wife, and the two will become one flesh'? So they are no longer two, but one. Therefore what God has joined together, let man not separate. (Matthew 19:4–6)

Through Facebook, I shared that verse to explain God's definition for a better way to deal with marriage, and I followed that with, "Don't attack gay marriage and don't try to defend what Jesus said. Jesus can defend himself. If you believe that Jesus loves people more than anyone else has ever loved people, then stick with his definition of marriage, and do not attack anyone whose views are different."

In short, my response was, "Don't attack anyone. Point toward Jesus. Love people."

Within a week, the message had been viewed by 57,782 people, picked up by three local newspapers, splattered on two front pages for Easter Sunday, and had received hundreds of comments. Based on what I wrote on Facebook, I had been told the following: "You're a hater. You're a blasphemer who misuses the words of Jesus for your own benefit. Gay people obviously aren't welcome at Flatirons."

The following comment was found on the web article written by a local newspaper: "Nero had the right idea." This user was referring to the Roman emperor Nero, who practiced mass genocide of Christians. And that comment was from the so-called tolerant, open-minded party.

None of that was a shocker. But the comments that were the most hurtful came from friendly fire. They were Flatirons people who, based on a paragraph from my Facebook page, decided that our community had turned our backs on grace, and they believed they'd never be welcomed again.

I would have expected that type of response from someone who had never attended a weekend at Flatirons, but *never* from someone who had been a part of our community for years.

At Flatirons, we have a slogan or phrase that we stand by called "Me Too." "Me Too" stands for the idea that we are all poor in spirit. We are all equal in our spiritual poverty. We don't have a list of sins that we ignore and another that we throw stones at. We've all broken links of the chain. "Me Too" represents what I think will be the most common conversation in anyone's first five minutes in heaven. When asked, "How did you get here?" we will all reply, "I screwed up my life, but Jesus cut me a sweet deal, paid my debt, and told me I could be with him forever."

And everyone in heaven will shout back, "Me too!"

In fact, the Flatirons phrase "Me Too" all started when Richard, the man I talked about in chapter 8, shared his struggle with homosexuality from stage during the weekend. When he was done, I took the stage and said, "I sure do love Richard, and I'm glad he's here," and a whole bunch of people from the crowd yelled back, "Me too!"

Ta-da! "Me Too" was born.

After I made that Facebook post, there were people from within the Flatirons community who began to say we'd turned our backs on "Me Too." I was blown away. I didn't get it. Did people not understand that everybody, at some time in their lives, wrestles with their own sexual issues and questions? Did people not understand that I have family members and people I love who are gay?

Did people not understand that I had searched the Bible for any verse or hint that opens the door for homosexual behavior or gay marriage to somehow fit within God's definition of what's best for a person?

Trust me, I've searched. And I can't find it. If I could teach that homosexual behavior was not a broken link in the chain, then my life as a preacher would be *so* much easier. If I could find that in the Bible, I would teach it in a heartbeat, and that goes for almost everything else I teach from stage. Why? Because every time I teach on the subjects of adultery, divorce, greed, selfishness, or homosexuality, they fall heavily on people that I *really* love. Sometimes the truth devastates them. Sometimes the truth devastates me.

There are so many truths in the Bible that I don't understand and will never pretend to. There's also some stuff in the Bible that I don't even like. I wish those things weren't in there. When I get to heaven, I will ask Jesus about these truths.

But until then, if I'm going to remain a devout follower of Christ, let alone a decent pastor, then I am constrained to preaching the truth I find in Scripture and nothing else. When I get to heaven, if Jesus decides to clarify his stance on homosexual behavior, then I refuse to look back at him and exclaim, "Oh no! I misunderstood you! That truth made me uncomfortable and it hurt people very close to me, so I changed it. I was trying to love people, but I'm afraid I made it worse."

That's why, as long as I continue to teach, I will be a target for both sides. During the social debate on civil union, many people asked me, "What if people leave Flatirons over what you say?"

I replied with the words of Paul from Galatians:

Am I now trying to win the approval of men, or of God? Or am I trying to please men? If I were still trying to please men, I would not be a servant of Christ. (Galatians 1:10)

If you choose to chase after God and hold to his truth without letting go of his grace, then you, too, will find yourself being shot at from both sides. As we've already read, Jesus guaranteed it in his first documented public talk.

If you hold to grace and truth, then you are called to love and welcome all people. But if we want to talk about equality, why don't we talk about the following?

All people are equal at the foot of the cross.

This doesn't mean that you can claim all behaviors, gay or straight, to be equally good or true. That would be ignoring truth. As a pastor, if I begin ignoring or tearing out any passage from Scripture that made me or someone I loved uncomfortable, then you should leave my church. If I begin ignoring some truths, then it's only a matter of time until I ignore all of them.

On the other side of that spectrum, we can't begin letting go of grace. If we do, the next thing you know, we will have religious whack jobs riding around American cities in the backs of pickup trucks, like they do in Kabul. They'll beat up people that they've deemed "sinners," and America will soon produce the Christian version of the Taliban. Historically speaking, that's the way truth without grace has always played out.

In my experience, I've found that teaching truth *with* grace causes people to run toward Jesus, not away from Jesus.

TRUTH, GRACE, AND NO MORE DRAGONS

Did Jesus love people? Yes.

Did Jesus ever change what his Father said was true? No.

But did Jesus ever throw stones at anyone who had fallen short of what his Father said was true? No.

Therefore, it is our job to figure out how to be full of both grace *and* truth. We have to figure out how to hold to truth without picking up stones. We also have to figure out how to hold to grace without lying to ourselves about our sin. We must mourn and be brokenhearted over our sin and what it has done to our relationship with God. But then we must allow God to put us back together so that we can be used to bring his kingdom of heaven to earth.

I can promise that holding to grace and truth will be better, but I can't promise it will be easier.

Think about your own story. Didn't it all fall apart when you let go of either truth or grace?

One day, you let go of truth, and you suddenly began believing things about yourself that weren't true. You began seeing a different version of yourself than God sees. You began valuing yourself differently than how God values you. You began thinking dragon thoughts.

Then somewhere down the line, you let go of grace. You couldn't see how God could ever forgive you. After all, you couldn't forgive yourself. You hated what you'd become, and you projected those feelings onto God. You were sure that he hated you too.

But there is hope, and his name is Jesus. Specifically, your hope can be found in the truth and grace that Jesus offers.

I started this book with the words from a twelve-step program: *Hi, my name is Jim, and I'm a dragon.*

The problem is that so many of us get stuck at the beginning of that statement: *Hi, my name is _____, and I'm a dragon.*

But if we were to begin placing our faith in Jesus' description of a better life, then the rest of that statement could sound so much better:

Hi, my name is _____, and I used to be a dragon. But because of the truth and grace of Jesus Christ, I've been set free. He reached into the scaly mess that had become my life and gave me a new start. I'm a new creation. The old has gone. The new has come. No more shame. No more regret. No more condemnation.

No more dragons.

NOTES

Chapter 1: You, Me, and Dragons
1. C. S. Lewis, *The Voyage of the Dawn Treader* (New York: HarperCollins, 2009), 97.
2. Ibid., 115.
3. Ibid., 117.

Chapter 2: Monkeys, Naked People, and Traitors
1. "Stairway to Heaven," lyrics by James Patrick and Robert Plant; recorded by Led Zeppelin, *Led Zeppelin IV*, 1971. Copyright Flames of Albion Music Inc.

Chapter 4: Elephants, Lions, and Depression
1. "Hurt," lyrics by Trent Reznor; recorded by Nine Inch Nails, *The Downward Spiral*, 1994.

Chapter 6: Prayer, People, and Pills

1. C. S. Lewis quote in *Shadowlands*, directed by Richard Attenborough (1993; Home Box Office Home Videos, 1998), DVD.
2. A. W. Tozer, *The Purpose of Man: Designed to Worship* (Ventura, CA: Gospel Light, 2011), 181.
3. From a personal conversation with Roy Mays.

Chapter 7: Missing Limbs, Burned Pizza, and Chreaster Services

1. *Dumb and Dumber*, screenplay by Peter and Bobby Farrelly, 1994.

Chapter 9: Scarred Guys, Sick Guys, and Small Steps

1. Dave Ramsey, *The Total Money Makeover: A Proven Plan for Financial Fitness* (Nashville: Thomas Nelson, 2009), 91. The original source for this quote is not known.

Chapter 10: Truth, Grace, and Spiritual Poverty

1. From the *Zodhiates* commentaries, s.v. *makarios*.
2. From the *Zodhiates* commentaries, s.v. "poor."

ACKNOWLEDGMENTS

Thank you to Robin, Alison, and Jordan for allowing me to run after Jesus and drag you down all of my rabbit trails along the way. Nothing is more important to me than us coming through this journey together, still loving each other, loving Jesus, and loving his church.

Thank you to my Mom and Dad, who introduced me to Jesus, opened their arms and their home to messy, lost, broken people, and never once told me that anything Jesus might want for my life was impossible.

Thank you to my elder team: Paul, Wayne, Keith, and Michel. I never thought it could be possible for a pastor to refer to his elders as his closest, most trusted friends . . . or to look forward to elders' meetings because they are some of the highlights of my week.

Thank you to Scott Nickell, my partner in teaching and leadership. I couldn't do this without you. I wouldn't want to try.

Thank you to Paul Brunner who constantly lifts me up, and Michael Koehn who constantly keeps me grounded.

Thank you to Randy and Chris, the other two-thirds of my creative brain.

Thank you to Ben Foote, husband to my daughter, father to my granddaughter, and the best and only editor who could take my ADHD manuscript and decipher it into something that makes sense.

Thank you to Dan Foote, my dive buddy who wouldn't stop saying, "You should write that down." Without you, I wouldn't have.

Finally, thank you to everyone who calls Flatirons their church. Together, we can do the things that Jesus wants us to do in the way that Jesus wants us to do them. Thank you for letting me have the greatest job possible.

ABOUT THE AUTHOR

Jim Burgen is the lead pastor of Flatirons Community Church. Over the past five years, Flatirons has been consistently named one of the most creative and fast-growing churches in America. Jim, along with a team of incredibly talented, gifted, and passionate teachers, artists, and servant-leaders, has dedicated his life and ministry to bringing the awesome life of Christ to a lost and broken world. Jim's passion is holding onto both truth and grace, eliminating religious obstacles and weirdness, and creating excellent and safe environments in which people can bump into Jesus.

Jim has authored several books, including *What's*

the Big Deal About Sex? (Standard Publishing)—a 2000 Gold Medallion Award Winner. He serves on the board of SOZO international, a non-government organization focused on relief and development in Central Asia. Jim also travels multiple times each year to Afghanistan, Uganda, and South Sudan in order to teach and learn from Flatirons's international partners.

Aside from Flatirons and its international partners, Jim can be found in the mountains hunting, shooting, hiking, camping, or four-wheeling. Jim lives with his wife, Robin, in Erie, Colorado. They are the proud parents of Alison and her husband, Ben, Jordan and his wife, Leah, and their grandchildren, Jonah and Emery. Completing the family is their spoiled yellow lab named Gertie.